TRAVEL
THE PLANET
OVERLAND

Graeme and Luisa Bell

TRAVEL THE PLANET OVERLAND
2nd Edition 2017

1st Edition 2016
Copyright © 2016 Graeme Bell

ISBN: 978-0-620-71990-2

Written by Graeme and Luisa Bell

Edited by Luisa Bell
Cover Photo by Graeme Bell
Graphic Design by Luisa Bell
Photos by Luisa and Graeme Bell

Disclaimer: The material in this book contains content/language of a mature nature. This book is written in the Queen's English with South African colloquialisms.

www.a2aexpedition.com
Instagram: graeme.r.bell
Instagram: a2a.expedition
Facebook: a2a.expedition

CONTENTS

Escapism

Escapism is an industry. Magazines, movies and ten million Instagram posts a day, dedicated to your dream of travel, of adventure and exploration. International tourism is a massive market accounting for US$ 1.5 trillion in 2015 alone and those are the receipts which were declared and taxed. Imagine the tourist spending, entering the pockets of informal traders and guides, hostels, hotels and street snack vendors. It is an industry based on your desire.

It is the carrot at the end of a very long stick.

What the tourism industry desperately peddles is a unique experience, a beautiful destination, an opportunity to live for a few weeks in a manner you would love to live your entire life. I don't know about you but I hate going on holiday, be it a drive down to the coastal resort for a couple weeks or a flight to some new exotic destination. I know that I hate it because I had been doing it wrong for many years. I loathe huge crowds of people, long queues and congested traffic. I despise people who are friendly to me only because of the dollars in my wallet and I detest returning home from a vacation financially drained and more exhausted than when I left. That kind of travel is like making love without achieving orgasm, wholly dissatisfying considering the effort it takes to get laid.

We broke the impotent vacation cycle when we bought an old Series Land Rover bakkie (pick-up). We threw a mattress in the bed of the bakkie, bought some sleeping bags and a cooler box and headed out into the mountains to camp for a weekend. It was bliss. We made a fire, grilled some meat, drank some of the good stuff and went to bed smiling. It was not the most comfortable weekend but we spent less than it takes to fill a tank with fuel. A love affair was rekindled. As the years passed we camped as often as possible and learnt some valuable lessons about gear, comfort and necessity. Every trip took us further and further away from home until eventually the travel became a priority. This is when the term overlanding entered our lives. We eventually plucked up our courage, took the children out of school for half a year and journeyed in our new, second hand Defender 130 from Cape Town, where we lived, to Tanzania and back, solo. We would never be the same.

Two years later, we left our native South Africa, having sold almost everything we had. We shipped our Defender to Uruguay and spent the next three years overlanding South America, eventually circumnavigating the beautiful continent, almost twice and visiting every country before driving up through Central America to Alaska and back down to Mexico. We made some terrible mistakes, got lost often, ran out of money, had a bunch of breakdowns and the time of our lives. All of the problems we had were school fees and I believe, despite our accomplishments, we have not yet graduated.

We have, however, discovered travel as a way of life, a nomadic existence which pushed us to the very edge of our capabilities and strengths and left us stronger and more capable. We discovered new lands and people, foods and cultures but, most importantly, we discovered ourselves.

This book is written to help you, "crack the code" of long-term overland travel, based on what we have learnt from the people we have met on the road, our failures, triumphs and our experiences travelling as a family of four. If you are planning to change your life, we have the tools to help you. However, this is not the overlanders Bible, it is his Pink Floyd, The Wall. Tear down the wall!

Disclaimer

This book will inspire you to get out there and go, whether for a weekend, a month or ten years. And while we are giving you all the crucial information you need to live the overlander dream, it is very important that you understand a few things, particularly if you plan to become a long-termer like us:

1. Perhaps the most important question you have to ask yourself before setting off to travel the planet is – why? Why do you want to leave behind the comforts of modern civilization, your friends, family and career for a path less travelled? Do you feel that you absolutely have to travel, do you want to impress your friends, family and colleagues. Do you want to live a life less ordinary and educate yourself, do you want to escape? Obviously one has to spend many hours in deep self-contemplation if you are to understand your own motivations and desires. The success of your journey may depend on a deeper understanding of those desires, wants and needs.

2. Overlanding is addictive. Once you get through the first few months on the road and into the rhythm, you may find that all other ambitions and long term plans become secondary to the goal of achieving a long-term overlander lifestyle.

3. Not everyone will be happy living the overlander lifestyle. You may read this book and think, 'Yes! I am going to do it', then start unravelling the life you have worked so hard to build. Stop! Take a month off and go on a road trip somewhere near but far. Live in a tent, count every penny. You might love the road or loathe it, the same applies to your companions (if any).

4. #VanLife is becoming very popular, even fashionable as is it's less mobile cousin, the #TinyHouseMovement. Both of these are a reaction to the exorbitant costs of living particularly in the North Western Hemisphere. Your social media accounts are no doubt full of beautiful images of little cabins in the country and VW Kombis on the beach. The reality is most likely a cluttered little house in a not so great neighbourhood or permanently being harassed by the cops for trying to sleep in your van by the beach or overheating trying to get up into the hills where you can camp for free. Wherever there is an interest, there will be people trying to cash in. Hipsters with beards down to their balls riding retro bicycles, while eating a gluten free croissant on the way back to their little van, where they will make 100 grand a year selling handmade axes, do not exist in the real world.

5. Overlanding full time is one of the greatest challenges you will ever take on in life.

You have been warned.

"And there are new kinds of nomads,
not people who are at home everywhere,
but who are home nowhere.
I was one of them"
Robyn Davidson

You might struggle to become an overlander if:

1. You whine a lot
2. You don't like bugs
3. You have never been camping
4. You look down on other cultures
5. You are petrified of your neighbouring countries
6. You don't like dirt
7. You are not patient or able to fake patience
8. You are unable to self-motivate
9. You are unwilling to try new things
10. You whine a lot.

Now that that is behind us, dig into this book and relish every page, you will find information that may change your life. Between these covers lie secrets. Find them!

Graeme and Luisa Bell

The Overland Tribe

Getting To Know the Different Types of Overland Travellers

There are generally four types of overland travellers roaming this planet, they are our tribe and we love them:

The Young Professional

Usually a couple of young professionals who are recently married or considering marriage. They may or may not have a dog. They do have some spare cash and an unscratched itch and generally travel in vans and 4x4's with rooftop tents or on motor bikes. They hike constantly and have wonderful, fulfilling sex lives. Very rarely a female young professional will travel solo but, more common, is the solo young male professional. The solo young male is a horny bugger who can often be found at a youth hostel surrounded by loosey goosey backpackers or taking selfies in front of canyons, mountains, glaciers and other tourist hot spots.

The Family

We fall under this category. Generally travelling in large 4x4s, vans, RV'S or trucks, the Family is all about the Family. And dishes; and chores; and maintenance; and home schooling; and money. Generally, in their late 30's or early 40's, the Family has been successful financially but seeks something more out of life. There is philosophy and risk and a constant tension under the surface. The Family is taking on a huge responsibility, rewriting the book on good parenting and trying to get the little monsters to brush their bloody teeth and maybe do some dishes if his or her majesty is quite finished sitting on their asses doing sweet blow all.

The Retired Couple

They might be retirement age or in their 50's, maybe even younger. They, like the family, generally travel in larger vehicles and can often be found sitting in the shade next to their massive Volvo truck, sipping on a gin and tonic, ice cubes and all, with a pair of binoculars and a birding book. They have the best toys - the kayaks, the motorbikes, quad bikes, even stuff that flies. They eat out a lot.

The Cyclist and the Biker

The two are not the same but carry limited gear and are the world's best recipients of a hand out. No space for firewood, grill, beer or steak? Here have some of mine. The cyclist will often return home after a gruelling year on the road with more money than when they left, whereas the biker will return with a droopy BMW. These two have the best contact with the geography and people they pass on the road.

• Honourable mentions. The sailors who travel the world by sea, risking pirates and skin cancer daily, aka Cruisers. Often overlanders become Cruisers when they realise how cheap it can be to live on a sail boat. Also, the public transport traveller, an overlander of sorts who lets someone else worry about mechanics and maintenance.

The first task on your list should be to decide which category you fit into. You will then be able to make the correct choices based on the style of travel which appeals to you most and fits your budget.

Long-terming can be either very expensive or dirt cheap, it all depends on where you are going and what you are prepared to do without. The key is to control your expenses, or overheads as they are called in the business world. If your income is greater than your overheads then you are on the path to success, if not, you are on the path to ruin. Most long-termers have limited resources and have to manage those resources well.

Bearing that in mind, here is another grossly generalised list of the different types of overlanders...

The Rich

There are those in this world who are born rich and buried rich, Old Money. Then there are those who worked their way to wealth, aka New Money. Usually the rich do not advertise their wealth, understandably. The whole world wants to be that kind of rich and most will do just about anything to achieve that status. These are the people who probably understand art and have old university friends and a house in France and one in San Francisco. They are different from you and I but no less lovely or terrible. Perhaps they should be respected if they would rather spend that money on an overland truck than another polo pony, property or sail boat. Often these people don't appear as you would expect, they do not wear golf shirts and chinos and ray bans, they do not all have long thin blonde bodies and the smile of a God. That girl with the old sandals and new computer, that could be her, or that guy on a bicycle tortured by a head wind in Patagonia, that could be him. You just don't and perhaps should not know. It will change the conversation, you will expect them to pay for dinner, it will ruin the friendship.

The Realtor

He or she bought a property or two in good neighbourhoods or close to the Israeli embassy in Berlin. They might have inherited the property or worked their fingers to the bone for twenty years to pay off the bank loan or they might have "flipped" properties for a profit. Either way they have reached a point where their income is greater than their forecasted expenses. Usually they will rent out a property or three and use the income to pay for their living and "back home" expenses. They will often be found travelling for long periods in developing nations where their Pound, Euro or Dollar buys five times what it would back home. (A couple living in a van can get by on $2000 dollars a month or even less depending on how tough, disciplined and frugal they are).

The Retiree

May be a combination of The Rich and The Realtor, or simply someone who has allotted his last ten active years to doing something worthwhile, living a lifelong dream before true old age sets in and screws everything up.

The Optimist

He or she are good at what they do. They know how to make money and have years of experience in their field, they are considered successful by their friends and family and have made their money by being an entrepreneur or a professional. They are not really sure how they will pay for the future but they are 87% sure that they will find a way. They might become English teachers or pack parachutes or find a pub to run down by the beach. Generally they are resourceful and intelligent. What more do you need? They believe in themselves, most of the time, and realise that they will have to stop and work again, sooner or later. The optimist runs the risk of becoming a Moocher.

The Moocher

These are the guys who arrive at a party with one bad bottle of wine and drink the good wine. They have no qualms taking food or accommodation or labour from others. They are forever staying in someone else's home, reluctantly camping in the garden or happily sleeping in the spare room, tapping into the WIFI. The Moocher has explained to himself that he is enriching the life of his host and should not feel guilty about eating another's food or making himself comfortable in their home. In a week or a month, they will be gone, they will leave a little gift and remember the hosts birthday. The Moocher is usually harmless and is generally a social person with many stories to tell. He may even offer to do the dishes once the dishes have been done. If you are reading this book and live close to an overlander route you would have most likely already met the Moocher. Cyclists and Bikers can sometimes be first class Moochers, they have a valid excuse.

The Short Term Long-Termer

These travellers fly in and fly out, leaving their rig for six months at a time while they return to whatever high paying part time job they have lined up back home. They tend to be very focused travellers with a plan and a route and a time frame. They range from academics to IT professionals and have perfected the art of having a cake and eating it.

The On The Road Worker

If you are clever enough to understand Search Engine Optimisation and e-commerce and have set up agreements with suppliers and are able to deliver nationally and internationally while holding minimal stock and employing minimal staff, this may be the path for you! Living in a developing nation reduces your private overheads significantly and while you have a connection to the internet you should be able to run your "first world" business remotely. This may involve keeping strange hours so that you are able to operate in "real" time with clients and suppliers on the other side of the planet but the upside is the view from your office is ever changing and you still get to live the dream, just a busy version. IT professionals who can work remotely are in the same boat, that boat just can't be too remote. If you are a chef or a cook or can bar tend and don't mind a flexible interpretation of immigration laws you could find yourself some income in tourist hotspots where English or European language speakers are desirable as short term, tax free "under the table" employees. You could also volunteer on ranches and farms where you won't earn any money but your day to day living expenses will be covered. There are many excellent work and travel resources available on the internet, (please read the chapter titled, Show Me the Money and the list of online resources at the end of this book).

The European on Sabbatical

With an excellent social welfare system and powerful currency, the Europeans really do have wonderful opportunities to travel without selling the farm. In France and Belgium, employees can take a year's paid sabbatical and will be guaranteed a job when they return. Other European countries have similar labour laws. Imagine that? A couple could easily fly to Brazil, buy a VW Kombi, which were still manufactured in Brazil until the last day of 2013, and drive all the way up to Alaska then sell the Kombi to a traveller headed the other way. Or they could fly to Johannesburg and buy a kitted Land Rover and drive it back home. One day, when I grow up, I intend to be European. "Research shows that wellbeing in working life for those on leave and the possibilities to be employed for the replacing persons are furthered by the leave system". In other words this "sabbatical" idea is actually beneficial for the employer, leave taker and replacement worker. The leave taker gets to relax and reflect and de-stress, perhaps study or otherwise improve themselves, the replacement worker gains experience and on the job skills and the employer gains happy, healthy, motivated workers. Socialism, the European overlanders very best buddy. There are a few quid pro quo's though. The worker has to have worked for the same employer for five continuous years and has to have at least ten years full time working experience. Naturally these laws and requirements vary from country to country so it is advisable that you do some research into the particular labour laws of your country, regardless of European Union membership. If you are not a European and intend to travel in ten years' time, migrate to Europe now.

Which type of traveller are you?

Now that you have had a good look at your resources, let's revisit the types of travellers and establish whether you are a Young Professional (solo or not), a Family, a Retired Couple, a Cyclist or a Biker. Let us work from the cheapest travel option to the most expensive.

The Cyclist

A Cyclist may be a Moocher but often that is by necessity and is usually acceptable as everyone understands that the long-term, long distance Cyclist is without doubt a bit of a nut job, masochistic with a guilty conscience and a bad childhood. Why else would they subject themselves to that torture? The only travelling option cheaper than being a Cyclist is to be a Walker but unless you are dragging a massive crucifix, everyone will just assume that you are homeless. A vehicle of any sort gives you a semblance of respectability. Dragging a massive crucifix will guarantee a warm bed and a hot meal every night unless you are dragging it through some parts of the Middle East, in which case your head will be on a spike - chop, chop.

The Cyclist Overlanding gear kit should include:

1. Advanced mooching vernacular of the region you will be travelling through
2. Vaseline to soothe private parts
3. Razors for leg shaving

4. A big, warm, weary smile
5. A small tent in case you don't come across a home to sleep in
6. A sleeping bag
7. 12 pairs of high quality underwear
8. Sexy padded lycra shorts x 2
9. Sexy lycra cycling shirts x 2
10. A raincoat
11. A warm jacket
12. Strong condoms
13. An iPod with some audio-books

You will be burning huge amounts of calories every day so make sure that you have a supply of energy bars and a bib for when you come across a plate of food. Watching an overland Cyclist eat is never pretty. Perhaps the greatest advantages of the bicycle as mode of adventure travel is that your body is the machine which keeps it moving, which will save you a fortune in fuel costs and bicycles can fly with you across the planet at very low cost, sometimes for free. Also, it is important to realise that you DO NOT have to cycle the entire route from A to B unless you intend to set a world record of some sort or make a documentary. In most countries you CAN cycle the passes and roads which are beautiful and warrant cycling, then take a bus or other form of transport to the next destination. There is no shame in it and you will ease your suffering significantly. This is a very good idea if you plan to cycle through mountainous or desert regions. DO NOT jump off a bus and cycle into Cuzco and pretend that you cycled the whole way. Other long-termers have a great nose for bullshit and once they sniff out your deception, you will be held over the coals.

The Biker

Bikers are the rock stars of the overland trail. They come bursting in making a god awful noise, dressed head to toe in leather, dirty and thirsty. I admire them greatly. Know this, if a biker or two comes blaarping into your camp and they spot that you have a campfire, or a beer, or a piece of meat, they will become your new best friend. They simply do not have the packing space for any of those luxuries and it would be rude of you not to share your bounty and let them store their gear under your truck.

A good Biker might have a small bottle of whiskey to add to the festivities which should endear them to you and soften the hunger pains after a shared plate. What motorbikes lack in terms of off-road and load carrying capabilities, they make up for with pure fun and excitement. At the end of the day the Biker is the happy man around the camp unless he took a tumble or spent the day riding through sand or mud. Then he is fast asleep after the first beer.

The Biker overlanding gear kit should include:

1. Basic mooching vernacular of the region you will be travelling through
2. Vaseline to soothe private parts
3. A big, warm, weary smile
4. A small tent in case you don't come across a home to sleep in

5. A sleeping bag
6. 12 pairs of high quality underwear
7. Sexy leather boots
8. Sexy riding ensemble in black and orange or red and grey or blue and grey
9. A helmet with built in comms, GoPro and speakers
10. Three, "I survived the whatsitwhatsit rally" t-shirts
11. A raincoat
12. A warm jacket
13. Extra strength condoms.

Bikers tend to be eat as you go types, they can find a cold beer and a deep fried snack in the middle of the Sahara, a couple of cans of sardines and some snack bread will be enough, in case a wild overnighter has to be endured with the exception of multi day off-road routes.

Unlike bicycles, motorbikes need to be shipped from continent to continent unless the adventurer intends to buy a bike in the first country off the plane. There are stories of bikers hitching rides on sea going vessels, and because motorbikes are relatively small, a resourceful Biker may be able to secure such passage at minimal comparable cost. This may be a rumour or once possible but now not.

The Young Professional

Let's assume that our YP's are a couple. They have been working for the last ten years and have check listed their twenties. It is time for the next phase but first they need to get out there and get some adventuring done before having babies and making money and building a bright golden future.
A word of warning, long-terming will kill a weak relationship. Time and again we have met a loving couple on the road who have split up as soon as they get back into the normal back home routines. A strong relationship will only grow stronger and marriage and babies are inevitable if our YP's are not already married. First they will need to decide on a suitable overland rig. Without kids or bad backs, the YP's can easily rough it with a mattress thrown on top of a platform in the back of a pick-up with a canopy. They can hang cargo nets and stuff all their stuff into crevices and have a few large Tupperware boxes for food and kitchen utensils, toiletries and clothes. He will find some space for a tool box and a few spares and they will spend the next year testing the static suspension of their rig. The YP's are young and curious and physically fit.

They will happily spend their spare time hiking up and down and around mountains and glaciers and cities. They will meet up with other YP's on the road and get up to all kinds of stupidity which will become the legend for other YP's to live up to. He will grow a beard and become soulful, she will jog everyday and become as fit as a fiddle. They both will change so much that when they return they will no longer be recognisable to their friends, who will quickly tire of their amazing stories. They did not realise when they began this journey that there is no way to go back to being normal.
You become a nomad, a wanderer, a free spirit. You become that weirdo who is always counting coins, never buying all the crap that all your friends spend their earnings on. Once the addiction has crept into your veins there is no way to get it out, no way to satisfy the beast but to get back

on the road where a veil lifts from your eyes and within a day you are happy again. The YP's thought they were just going for an adventurous drive. Their lives will never be the same again.

The YP's overland gear kit should include:

1. Bottles of whisky, tequila and wine stashed throughout the truck
2. Sunscreen and good hiking boots
3. A year's supply of birth control and a reminder written on the windscreen
4. An external hard drive full of their favourite movies and TV shows
5. Two iPods, fully loaded
6. Yoga pants for her, lumberjack shirts for him
7. 12 pairs of underwear each
8. Disposable clothing
9. Disposable bedding
10. A plan for the purchase and storage of Marijuana (note, we do not encourage the use of drugs, hard or soft).

YP's do not usually have the resources to travel indefinitely, but they will have to find a way. There really is no going back to "normal".

The Family

By far the busiest of all the long-termers. These poor fools hardly ever get a rest while essentially trying to run a household and raise children. The French, of all nations, seem the best equipped for raising families on the road and they tend to have large families with a minimum of four children. They do not pander to the kids who are aware of their duties and responsibilities around the camp. Polish kids are absolute nutters who run amok screaming at the top of their lungs while looking for stray dogs to kick in the balls. American kids are constantly photographed, parents shadowing them like paparazzi, their every movement cataloged and blogged about while South African kids refuse to do their home schooling and would rather help a stranger set up his camp and rebuild his Toyota engine before helping Mom with the dishes. Ah, to be French. They drink alcohol with most meals which are organic vegetables and salads and fruit and pasta. The children clean up and take care of each other while the adults tell interesting jokes and plan the afternoons activities. So slim, so normal, so annoying.

The Family is trying to reinvent the wheel while living a life less ordinary, packed into tight spaces and enduring each other 24 hours a day. Most Families long-term travel before their children are of school going age but the truly insane try and raise their children on the road. In Germany it is illegal for children to not go to school, the French have a very strict schooling syllabus to fulfil while the South African authorities don't give a shit what you do about education as long as you give them a nice big pile of Romany Cream biscuits when they inspect your home before you leave to live in a car. Having little ones does increase the Families risk while travelling, a sick child or an accident is a catastrophe for which the parents will be eternally responsible regardless of fault. The child's entire future depends on their formative years, the education they receive when young, the certificates they will earn. The conservative may ask what these children are doing living outdoors, growing up surrounded by people who have given it all up to explore the planet? What does this unrooted lifestyle teach them? Preposterous, they should be in school, seven to two, five days a week, they should be doing what everyone else does. Homeschooling will be dealt with in another chapter.

Chill the wine.

The Overland Family gear kit should include:

1. Very heavy books, thirty of each to cover every subject for the two or three years you will be on the road
2. A wooden spoon, for stirring huge pots of pasta and threatening violence
3. A huge pot
4. Large and well thought out medical aid packs. Cyclists, Bikers and random strangers will treat your truck like a moving clinic. You have kids therefore you must have band aids and Ibuprofen
5. 12 pairs of underwear for each member of the family. 20 for teenage boys
6. A large and unwieldy box of toys, Lego, paints and crayons
7. Industrial size tubs of sunscreen
8. An infinite supply of patience
9. No desire to ever finish a sentence
10. Whatever alcohol you can get your hands on.

The Retired Couple

We will focus first on the elderly Retired Couple or RC and then the Early Retired Couple or ERC. The RC have worked hard their entire lives and are now soaking up every last drop of sunshine and beauty. No bird will be allowed to pass without appreciation and supermarkets will be scoured for Schweppes tonic which will then be bought wholesale. The RC has all the time in the world and will often drive in gigantic circles spending years in a region which appeals to them. Mr. RC will have an impeccable vehicle, cleaned regularly and maintained within the manufacturers specifications regardless of the cost.

He will spend his days driving where Mrs. RC tells him to and his evenings trying to sneak off for a few beers. Mr. RC wants meat and bread with butter and bacon and eggs, potatoes and chocolate and croissants. Mrs. RC feeds him lettuce and carrots and high fibre everything and prune juice. Mrs. RC is a love. Her blogs are flowery and poetic, she enjoys nothing more than a beautiful vista, a sighting of a wild beast, a day spent in the warm sunshine with Mr. RC at her side. Mrs. RC will spend hours every day planning the route, pouring over maps, dressed in khaki, feeling quite the adventurer. Her one regret is that she cannot spend more time with her grandchildren. She will have to be satisfied with the regular evening Skype session, a time which Mr. RC always seems to exploit to hang out with those foreign boys and drink beer. She just knows he is eating meat with them, his flatulence always takes on a different scent when he eats red meat.

The Retired Couple Overland gear kit should include:

1. High powered binoculars and a few birding books
2. First class medical insurance
3. Pharmaceutical prescriptions with translations into relevant languages
4. 3 map books, 10 guide books and a bilingual dictionary
5. Spare reading glasses
6. 12 pairs of underwear each
7. Pretty floral sheets and kitchen towels and camping chairs
8. Gin and Tonic
9. A vegetarian cookbook
10. Rubbing salve.

The ERC

The ERC has designed their own rig from the ground up, usually as a collaboration, where he does the technical research, planning and design, while she focuses on aesthetics. They then work together to build the rig while outsourcing the most technical aspects to professionals. Or they might buy the vehicle ready built. (Generally the more expensive factory made rigs won't make it out of North America or Europe. Those who can afford a half million dollar rig are not too interested in taking it too far from civilization. It is good enough that the vehicle can go anywhere theoretically, it does not actually have to prove it). Their clothing will be waxed oilskin from Fjallraven and their shoes will have been tested on Mars.
The ERC are usually a nice couple, eager to make friends, try new foods and have fun. They have the budget for all the touristy shit that The Family has to forego because they cannot afford to pay for five tickets at full price to look at another bloody waterfall. The ERC is forever meeting up with friends and family, renting apartments and flying around the planet for weddings and a change of scenery. The ERC are not always stupidly wealthy but they are wealthy enough. Neither the ERC or RC will ever be a Moocher but they do have the potential to complain the balls off an elephant.

The ERC you will meet in developing nations has the most sublime gear including but not limited to:
1. Panasonic Toughbook
2. A drone
3. A KTM 990 for popping down to the shops
4. A paramotor
5. A $20 000 DSLR
6. An inflatable boat with a 175 HP outboard engine
7. Satellite TV
8. Satellite Wi-Fi
9. Self-inflating tyres
10. A built in pizza oven

*There are long-termers who are a variation of all the travellers listed above. These are the Anomalies and they tend to puzzle the other groups.

HOW TO MOTIVATE YOUR

Often we meet people as we travel who would love to explore as we do but have one serious problem: their spouse hates camping. Or to be more specific: "my wife hates camping". If this is your problem then we suggest that you try the following Travel Indoctrination Campaign, or TIC, utilising the Behaviour Modification Training or BMT, before progressing with your overland planning. It would be a shame to go through all the expense and effort of building the perfect overland vehicle and planning the most amazing overland route and not being able to get that special someone out of the house.

The BMT will include elements of Neuro Linguistic Programming, NLP and will be purely Carrot based, as it is unadvisable and

SIGNIFICANT OTHER

unproductive to use the Stick method.

The TIC will not be cheap or quick and will require significant effort on your part but, once you have done the preliminary leg work and established a rhythm, you will find that the TIC will be successful beyond your wildest dreams. For the purposes of this exercise we will assume that the stubborn significant other is female.

Step 1

1. Tell Sweetie Pie that you are taking her for a romantic weekend
2. If you are further encumbered by children, arrange to have them stay at Grannies for the weekend
3. When she asks where you are going to take her tell, Noo Noo, that it will be a surprise

4. Ensure that your vehicle is pre-packed with an easy erect tent, a few candles, good dry firewood, a big soft mattress and big soft camping chair, champagne and pre-prepared food (her favourite)
5. Do not take any more than you absolutely need to; ensure that the weather forecast is good
6. Be prepared and do not expect Smooshie to do anything but be pampered
7. Be sure to arrive an hour before nightfall at an organised camp close to home, not too close to water or low income / high volume people
8. Make Butter Muffin a small fire and quickly set up the camp, while she sits back with a glass of champagne in her hand
   - Hold her close while the sun sets
   - Feed her the food
   - Have a deep and meaningful conversation about whatever she wants discuss
   - Lay her down on the soft mattress and make love to her gently but vigorously, the way she likes it
   - Feed her strawberry centred chocolate
   - Wake her up with a flower and a cup of tea or coffee, pack up quickly and take her to a cozy restaurant for breakfast
   - After a nice drive and a few hours spent looking at curios, buy her something beautiful
   - Arrive at a romantic getaway lodge where Shnookums can have a pedicure, then dinner
   - Later lay her down on the soft bed and make love to her vigorously, the way she likes it
   - Feed her strawberry centred chocolate (with all the lovemaking neither of you will need to worry about putting on weight)
   - Stay two nights
   - On the way home affirm, "camping isn't that bad, is it?", Pookie will agree and nod off.

Step 2
- You will need to plant little "programmers" around the house
- The beautiful curios will be placed on her nightstand, the last thing she sees before falling sleep and the first thing she will see when she wakes
- Brochures of five star camping or "glamping" scattered around the living room
- Conde Nast Traveller in the loo magazine holder
- Schedule travel programmes on the TV, focus on white beaches, palm trees and hammocks
- Be subtle but be consistent
- Twice a week, make love to her vigorously
- Feed her strawberry centred chocolate
- Bring her flowers often, put them in a vase on a table, next to a new travel magazine
- She will become suspicious of all the attention. Tell her that you love her and you are trying to be the best MAN you can be. (A MAN does manly things, a husband does what he is told, she does not need to know this definition and you need to find the balance).

Step 3
- Within two weeks, she will remind you of that wonderful weekend. This is the moment you have been waiting and preparing for
- Whisk Pooh Bear away and repeat that first weekend but camp for two nights then one night in a little cabin
- Each night lay her down on the soft mattress and make love to her vigorously
- Feed her strawberry centred chocolate.

Observation: Your wife will be happier and a happy wife is a happy life, so they say. She will be gloating to her friends and your relationship will improve significantly.

Not a bad thing.

Step 4
- Continue the Travel Indoctrination Campaign, or TIC, remembering to be subtle
- Take Cuddle Bug camping once a month, introducing one child at a time
- Feed her the chocolate.

After three months you will be able to measure her Residual Recreation Resistance, or RRR. Adapt the TIC accordingly. Within a year, Munchy Munch will be sleeping in a hammock on a river boat sailing down the Amazon. Make love often and continue feeding her the chocolate.

Choosing an Overland Vehicle

By now you should have an idea of which type of traveller you are to be and we would hopefully have given you enough information to decide by which means you will travel. Here are a few tips to help you narrow down your options and help you to make the correct choice of vehicle and gear.

The Bicycle

Choosing a bike can be daunting and it will be very easy to overspend, especially since bicycles can cost more than cars these days. Have a look at the countries and continents you intend to explore and assess the most common terrain. Will you spend most of your time on gravel or paved road, on open plains or in the mountains? Cyclist friends have told me that sometimes the best bike is whatever bike is locally available. You want something lightweight and easy to repair, minimal gears and a chain, never a belt. You have to then consider your luggage options. Saddlebags over the front and rear wheels are an option as well as a small trailer which you could pack with all your gear or a small, precocious child. You need good camping gear and a small reserve of food. The world is much smaller than it used to be and there are people almost everywhere and where there are people there is usually food. Eat what the locals eat but prepare for the inevitable gastro on the side of the highway.

Safety is a major concern for cyclists. You want to be as visible as possible. The safest way to travel by bicycle is to buy a car. But, if you insist, we suggest equipping your bicycle for maximum visibility. A couple of kinetic powered LED lights should illuminate your rear as well as a large luminous flag on a pole, in the front another light should be mounted. Your clothing should be luminous as well as your luggage. You want to be mistaken for a mullet wearer from the 80's. Never ride at night and always wear a helmet. It seems logical to ride against the traffic in order to see the dangers approaching but cyclists are not logical, therefore a rear view mirror is employed by most so that death can be seen approaching from the rear. Actually, in developing nations the bicycle is as ubiquitous as the motorcycle as it is the cheapest form of transport and as such, drivers tend to be aware of cyclists simply because you could be their brother, sister or uncle; that won't mean you will not have some close calls.

Since your body is the machine, you will not need to worry about fuel tanks but be sure to carry plenty of water and electrolytes for rehydration. There was once a German who cycled Patagonia and decided to use the constant one way tail wind to further advantage by fixing a sail to his bicycle. This bit of genius could bite you in the butt when an eighteen wheeler blows past you and sucks you into a vortex which will inevitably end with you scraping along the pavement leaving a trail of skin, blood and luminous socking, but, because you are a cyclist, you like falling down and spending hours picking grit out of your roastie scabs. So, enjoy the action.

Before leaving for your adventure, it is advisable to do some long distance touring. This is a great time to thin your luggage and talk yourself out of choosing a bicycle for an adventure. If you are going to take a buddy with you, ensure that your relationship is strong, that you have similar vices, are equally fit and healthy and have very similar expectations of the journey. If you do buddy up then you will be able to share the load of tools and spares. You can share a tent if you are also having sex with each other, otherwise it is better to have your own space, a bit of privacy can go a long way to keep the friendship fresh.

The Motorbike

One of the worst corporate mistakes made in the last fifty years was when some chop at KTM turned down Ewan McGregor and Charlie Boorman and sent them straight into the warm Germanic arms of BMW. Another is whenever a company turns down our request for gear, we wouldn't ask if we didn't need it, man! Anyway, I am sure KTM had their reasons but BMW has sold billions of motorbikes in the last decade thanks to our Scottish and English friends, you will have to wait a long time for a KTM to roll into camp while surrounded by Beemers. I would personally choose the KTM but I really have no idea what I am talking about, having not ridden many bikes since I destroyed my right leg on a Yamaha 1100cc almost twenty years ago, but that is another story for another time. Many overland Bikers are happy to ride the big 1200cc bikes but they are not cheap, a new model could cost as much as a good second hand Land Rover or Land Cruiser. Developing nations love the motorbike, it is the new donkey and a wise person might consider buying the top seller in the market they will be riding through, knowing that spares will be cheap and plentiful and that they could sell the bike at the end of the journey. However, the bikes favoured most in Asia, Africa and South America tend to be low cc runabouts so you might find yourself wanting for horse power when fully loaded. That said, I have seen a 250cc Honda carrying three adults and a pig at a decent speed.

Do yourself a favour, watch that Top Gear Vietnam special where the blokes ride a bunch of scooters across the country. If you want cheap thrills then that is the way to go. What could be better than buying a bike that costs less than a bicycle back home and whizzing your way around a continent or two with an old back pack strapped to the back seat and a pair of aviator goggles strapped to your Moto X helmet from 1984? When you break down, you can walk into any bike shop and walk out with the part you need or the locals will be able to fix the bike with WD40 and some bailing wire and you won't pay your weight in gold for either the labour or the spares. You could even hire a tuk-tuk, spray it a hundred different colours and convert the rear seat into a bed.

Which brings us to the modern machines. With more technology and rider aids than the Apollo craft had for the astronauts, you are sure to have a great time, if you enjoy power and speed and technical off-road touring. Bear in mind though, a long distance overland journey is not the same creature as that ride you took with your mate Paul from London to Scotland. Travelling through developing nations can become challenging when you need specialised service and parts. That said, modern bikes are designed to be reliable and dependable machines capable of going further perhaps than you are willing to. You will also be able to ride at very high speeds which increases the need for specialist protective clothing and a large, sturdy pair of balls. The Pan American highway is perfect for these powerful bikes particularly the high altitude mountain passes of Peru, where the endless switchbacks and curves will keep you grinning all day long. I have said it before but, if ever man was to inhabit Mars, the Peruvians should be contracted to build the roads.

The 4x4, Motorhome, Truck and Family Station Wagon

These four modes of transportation are very different yet very similar, hence we have decided to discuss them as one group. Perhaps the most significant difference is that motorhomes are generally purchased as an established, outfitted touring vehicle whereas the overland 4x4 and trucks are usually customised significantly by the owner, according to their specific requirements.

The family station wagon is difficult to modify with the exception of a roof rack and maybe a drawer system of some sort but is, surprisingly, a great vehicle for overlanding provided you don't intend to encounter too much rough stuff or intend to carry a lot of gear. The rear seats can be folded down for ample sleeping room for a couple and you can travel incognito at highway speeds and all the comfort of a trip to the grocery store. A Volvo V50 station wagon or a small delivery van would be perfect for travelling the planets major routes. The obvious limitation is the off paved road and load capabilities of these vehicles and the living space they provide. They say that you can drive from London to Cape Town in a Mini Cooper, think about that. Look out your window at whatever car you have parked in the drive way. You could probably drive that car most of the way around the world or at least from wherever you are to the furthest coastline.

Motorhomes are usually two wheel drive vehicles though there are a few exceptions like the 4x4 Sprinter and the VW Syncro but generally a motorhome is designed with gentle European and North American road tripping in mind. The Westfalia is truly loved by those who drive them, they often have a surf board or two strapped to the roof and orange curtains in the window. They break down a lot. The Iveco 4x4 van is also a popular base for a motorhome and though the owner will swear he can go anywhere your Land Rover can, he cannot. He will get stuck and you will have to drag his top heavy, low bellied beast out of whatever his ego got him stuck in.

Overland trucks are the Mac Daddys of the overland community. They promise huge ground clearance, massive living space, terrible gas mileage and exorbitant fees to transport across the oceans and through toll gates. Changing a flat tyre on the road can take a Herculean effort and replacing all tyres will cost the GDP of Bangladesh, but with a payload of several tons you will be able to take all your favourite toys with you. There probably is no better seat to sit in to see the world go by. Trucks are made for long distance driving and the comfort and visibility of the driver is carefully considered, those big padded bouncy seats, efficient air conditioning, heating and commanding ride height must make almost any journey a joy. You know those huge trucks they use in the Dakar rally, those awesome beasts which blast over the dunes and through the jungle and down the slopes and up the hills? These are not those trucks. The overland truck looks similar but weigh as much as the ocean when it still had fish in it. They do not cruise through the dunes and will not be seen on any but the most compact of beaches. They promise maximum freedom and comfort but deliver half of the one and all of the other.

The 4x4 is probably the most versatile base for a long or short term overland journey. How complicated your set up is, depends on a number of factors, not least your budget. Southern

Hemisphere overlanding can quite easily be done in a standard 4x4, equipped with a roof top tent and simple storage system for tools, clothes, spares, food, water and beer. The Northern Hemisphere tends to be less accommodating in terms of climate and anyone considering long-term overlanding in the upper half should consider some type of "live in" arrangement.

Choosing your vehicle may be as easy as buying the first good cheap model you find. Then there are those who are brand loyal. We love Land Rovers and have owned a few but eventually settled on the Defender 130 because of the large pay load. And because it is a Defender. That does not mean that we did not consider all the brands of 4x4's and different types of vehicle available. When making a long term decision it is always best to decide using your head not your heart. We looked at Toyotas, Nissan Patrols and Unimogs and other platforms before finally settling on the Defender.

Many of the following factors can also relate to motorhomes, trucks and even motorbikes...

FUEL TYPE

Diesel or gasoline or vegetable oil

Diesel is generally cheaper than gasoline and diesel vehicles tend to achieve much better mileage per litre than gasoline powered vehicles. A diesel vehicle with a low range gear box, has plenty of power and torque for off-roading and diesels tend to run a lot better through deep water.

Gasoline vehicles tend to be faster and a bit easier to drive. In many urban areas, gasoline is readily available where diesel is not.

Vegetable oil powered vehicles are an interesting option; the only problem is finding large amounts of old vegetable oil. I have a Chilean friend who drove a vegetable oil powered Land Rover Series 3 up and down the spine of South America. He had to have a few extra storage tanks built which sat up on the roof rack. He would approach fast food joints and ask them if he could have the old oil from the fryers and was usually successful. The simple beauty of this type of fuel is that you are doing less damage to both the environment and your wallet. The downside is that you fill the air with the scent of fries wherever you go and stray dogs find your rig irresistible. This friend called his Landy Gordo Fritangero, deep fried fat

MANUAL OR AUTOMATIC TRANSMISSION

As with all things, both transmission systems have their pros and cons.

A manual system gives the driver more precise control of the engine revolutions, speeds and, apparently, a manual gearbox is easier to field repair than an automatic "box".

An automatic vehicle is easier to drive particularly in high density traffic and in certain off-road conditions.

In deep sand and cloying mud, an automatic box can change quickly through the gears without losing that all important momentum. Modern automatic transmissions have a manual component which provides the driver with similar gearing as a manual transmission.

The most significant difference between the two is that a manual vehicle can be push started while the automatic vehicle has to be started by its own battery. If you are the type of person who often has electrical issues, then perhaps a manual vehicle would be better suited. We have, on a few occasions, had batteries fail in remote places. Because our Defender has a manual box and Luisa has good, strong legs we have always been able to get rolling to the next large town where we could find the fault.

Cruise control is a definite plus for those very long driving days on arrow straight roads.

Given the option, we would choose a manual vehicle over an automatic but that might have something to do with the fact that we were raised driving like men, stick in hand.

LEFT HAND DRIVE (LHD) VS RIGHT HAND DRIVE (RHD)

66% of the world drives on the right hand side of the road therefore 66% of the world's drivers drive LHD vehicles. It stands to reason then that if you have a choice between LHD and RHD for long-term international overlanding, LHD is the way to go. We have a RHD vehicle and it has been a huge pain in the butt, especially when overtaking. I have to rely on my family members to tell me when it is safe to overtake, the problem is that Luisa is a nervous Nelly, my son has never driven on a paved road and my little daughter has to make an effort to see over the dashboard. We have a system though. Here is the scenario... We are stuck behind an overloaded eighteen wheeler truck on a winding single lane road and the sun is setting directly in front of us. I will move the vehicle towards the centre line and whoever is in the passenger seat will crane their necks to have a look at the road ahead. If there is oncoming traffic they must say NO, if the road is clear they must say CLEAR. They may not say GO because GO sounds just like NO in a noisy Land Rover. Before this system became a habit we had more than a few near misses when I understood NO to be GO and headed out into the oncoming traffic to overtake. My navigator must also tell me how many vehicles are visible in the oncoming lane. Often they will tell me, 'There are two cars, a bus then a red truck, it might be clear after the truck'. They tell me the colour of the last vehicle so that I can easily identify it when it passes.

The problem with this system is that I, as the driver, am almost always reliant on someone else to be wide awake and participating. If the family falls asleep on a long road, I have to wait until the road conditions change enough that I am able to see the oncoming traffic and safely overtake.

The other drawback is that there are a few countries which do not allow RHD vehicles to cross their borders. This can be a massive problem when that country is en route to your destination and there is no way around it. In some cases special RHD permits may be obtained but often not. One solution is to have the RHD vehicle transported on a flat bed truck through the offending country but that is both expensive and obstructive as you will not be able to explore at your own pace. Also consider the following...

There are 34% of countries which drive on the left hand side (most of these are former British colonies) including Southern and East Africa, India, British Guyana, a few Asian countries and Australia. Driving on the left hand side is the correct side to drive on because that is where the Queen drives her Land Rover Defender

There exist vehicles with interchangeable LHD, RHD configurations such as the Mercedes Unimog and, with huge expense, your vehicle may be customised to do the same

Bear in mind that the headlights of RHD and LHD vehicles differ as they are designed to shine on the road ahead and the shoulder while not blinding oncoming traffic. There are special lens stickers which may be applied to the headlight outers for exactly this reason but it is recommended to install LHD headlights on RHD vehicles given the probability of driving with the other 66%. While you are doing that, install LED bulbs and a relay so as not to burn out the headlight switch (this applies specifically to Tdi and Td5 Defender drivers).

RHD in LHD countries (and vice versa) can present problems when stopping to pay at toll booths and when pulled over by the police. Corrupt police may insist that your vehicle is incorrectly configured and therefore illegal, a fine must be paid, a very, very big fine or the vehicle will be impounded. Do not fall for that. If you drove the vehicle into the country the policeman probably has no short, chubby leg to stand on.

SPARE PARTS

There is a reason why the most common 4x4 overland vehicles are Land Rover Defenders and Toyota Land Cruisers. Neither vehicle is indestructible but both have a dedicated fan base and a network of enthusiasts and dealerships throughout the planet. Land Rover discovered Africa and Toyota keeps it running, or so they say, that does not mean that you will easily find the parts that you need outside of the major commercial centres. But, with the modernisation of the developing world and the growth of the internet, the planet has shrunk considerably. DHL operates in 220 countries as does Fedex (which is incredible considering that the mighty Internet insists there are only 196 countries on our planet) and through a network of subsidiaries, are able to deliver almost anything, almost anywhere. You will pay for the privilege and may wait a month but eventually your part will arrive on the back of a donkey or in the hand of a fellow overlander and you will be able to get moving again. In the good old days adventurers needed back up teams, porters and a huge amount of gear to travel to far flung corners of the planet.
Mostly, those days are gone.

Memorise your vehicles VIN (Vehicle Identification Number) and take the time to understand what the numbers and letters represent. Using your VIN number when ordering parts will help to ensure that you receive the part you need for model vehicle.

Research the various after-market suppliers of parts, for your vehicle and use the supplier with the best reputation for quality and customer service.

Spare parts purchased directly from the vehicle manufacturer will generally be high quality but stupidly expensive. After-market parts naturally have varying degrees of quality and the price usually reflects that though some suppliers are more expensive than others.

Original Equipment "OE" – Parts made by the original manufacturer, as installed in a new vehicle on the assembly line

Original Equipment Manufacturer "OEM" – Parts that are manufactured to the same specs as the original part but without quality control tests or original logo on either the part or the packaging

After-market – Essentially "grey" parts with no clear guarantee of quality, which might range from great to absolutely terrible

Many countries have enthusiast clubs and they are an excellent source of information, particularly for local spares suppliers. Land Rover clubs are passionate and can be extremely helpful but do not expect anything more than friendship, guidance and perhaps hands on assistance. If you are going to be travelling to distant countries, you should have the resources to provide for your own repairs and maintenance without becoming a financial burden on strangers. Make an effort to meet up with enthusiast clubs even if you do not have an emergency, usually you will have a great time hanging out with them and sharing your stories

It is easy to pack too many spares and Murphy's Law dictates that the spares you do not have will be the spares you need. Again, get to know your vehicles strengths and weakness and prepare accordingly

Catalogue your spares and update the list when parts are used or added

If by some lucky miracle you come across a fellow traveller with an identical vehicle in desperate need of a spare you are carrying, calculate the replacement cost, including postage, and let them buy it from you at that cost, unless it is a low value item. You will help that person out and can make arrangements for a replacement at a later stage

Some countries have very strict customs regulations with regards to the importation of vehicle parts. You may find that on top of the cost of the part and the courier fees, you may need to pay an import duty on the value of the part. Sometimes that duty could be as high as 80%. If you are in this situation, it may be possible to have an invoice issued for the part at a much lower value, the duty will then be calculated at a lower cost

If using a courier to import essential parts, establish whether you can be refunded the import duties when driving out of the country. The courier may need to issue a specific invoice such as a "tourist invoice" and you may need to prove to the customs officials that you are leaving the country with the new part. This may be difficult if the part is an internal mechanism.

ESSENTIAL GEAR

In preparation for your journey you will no doubt visit REI or Cape Union Mart or Bass Pro Shops or whichever "adventure" retailer has the market share in your country. There you will be seduced by a vast array of products, each undeniably essential, and equally desirable. From water filters to solar torches, fire starters, carabiners, deep Arctic sleeping bags to inflatable pillows, collapsible cooking equipment, solar ovens, sporks and Frisbee plates, all will tempt you. Chances are you will already have a decent collection of gear sitting at home, a collection which you started assembling when you were 11. Do yourself a favour, resist the temptation, keep the money in your pocket.

You need to be ruthless when sorting your gear, perhaps have an itemised "definitely maybe" box, which you can leave with a relative or friend who can then post the box to you if you feel that you simply cannot live without the measuring cups, juicer and curling iron. Remember, wherever you travel in the world there will be stores which stock life's essentials.

Whittle your gear down to the following ...

Cooking equipment

Pots and pans
- A good set of preferably metal handled, non-stick pots and pans relevant to the size and appetite of your cooker and travel companions if not travelling solo
- Non-stick cookware uses less water, soap and effort to clean
- A colander, collapsible if possible. The colander can be used in conjunction with a similar size pot and it's lid to steam vegetables which reduces the use of both energy resources and water as you will only need to boil a small amount. Steamed vegetables also retain crispness and nutrients
- A pressure cooker – you want to be as efficient as possible with both your energy resources and time. A pressure cooker doubles the power of your heat source as it uses both that and the steam produced in the cooking process

A good quality set of non-stick friendly utensils including...
- A wooden spoon for stirring and serving
- A spatula

Basic kitchen tools including...
- A bottle opener
- Good quality potato peeler
- Tea strainer
- A can opener (the old school metal type is most reliable)
- A large cutting knife (Tiktaalik produces a great range of low profile, high quality kitchen knives)
- A knife sharpener
- A set of knives and forks, metal not plastic, pack plenty of GPS chipped teaspoons
- A suitable, easy to reach storage system for your utensils
- Metal mugs and plastic cups. If you are a wine drinker, find a safe place to store a good thick glass or even a mason jar. No one likes drinking wine out of plastic or metal cups.

- Mason jars are sturdy and cheap to replace and can also be used for storage
- A whistle kettle. When busy around camp, you may forget you had a kettle boiling, only to return to find a lot of gas and water wasted
- A set of plates, either plastic or wood. Plastic does not retain the heat of food and wood requires extra effort to clean. Only truckers take the good China on the road
- Paper plates are convenient for quick, on the go meals and can be easily disposed of and are eco friendly
- A large square container for washing dishes and carrying water. Square packs easier than round, in fact, everything should be as square as possible
- A funnel. Two of. One for the missus and one for you to use for topping up and transferring vehicle oils
- Aluminium foil, plastic wrap and lots of ziplock bags. Ziplock bags have a multitude of uses and can be resealed and washed and reused.

Braai / BBQ Equipment

You will be making plenty of fires for warmth, pleasure and cooking meat and vegetables. One of the best braai's we ever ate was made by Argentine Hippy Vegetarians in Peru.

1. A foldable braai grill. Remember this will need to be packed outside the vehicle or have it's own carry bag. After a few months of consistent use, the grill will mostly be coated with grease and grit, you do not want it bouncing around in the back of the rig, fouling everything
2. A grill brush to clean off said grease and grit once the grill has heated sufficiently over the coals
3. A good sturdy set of tongs for moving wood and flipping meat and vegetables
4. Braai fanatics can carry their own small stand alone stainless steel braai which uses less fuel than conventional campfires and can be used almost anywhere
5. Sosatie skewers, particularly the large Brazilian variety are fantastic for the easy flipping and cooking of a variety of food stuffs. They clean easily, are lightweight and pack away snugly. They can also be used for impromptu sword fights, depending on how much beer you drink.

The Cooker

You are going to be spending a lot of time cooking your own food while on the road. Your cooker must be up to the job. By far the most reliable source of fuel is propane which is also known as Liquid Petroleum Gas, or LPG. Cyclists and Bikers can use little camping stoves to heat up their cans of spaghetti or baked beans and for the morning cup of coffee. Overlanders in larger vehicles have more space, therefore more options, ideally you want a two burner with enough surface area to accommodate two pots or a pot and a frying pan. A good tip is to measure the circumference of the pots and pans which you intend to travel with and to buy a cooker accordingly or vice versa. Depending on your remoteness, frugality and number of passengers while travelling, you may use the cooker twice or even three times a day. A badly designed cooker will frustrate you endlessly, rather spend less on gadgets and gizmos and more on an appliance which will, without doubt, be used regularly.

Cooking fuel

LPG burns clean with consistent heat but, while LPG may be the most reliable source of fuel it may also be the most difficult to source. There are cookers which can run on dual fuel, ie, unleaded gasoline and "white gas" such as the infamous Coleman Dual Fuel stove. Finding unleaded gasoline is much easier than finding LPG but the dual fuel cooker burns dirty and produces a large amount of carbon monoxide which could prove lethal if used in confined spaces with limited ventilation. The Coleman Dual Fuel stove requires patience and a strict adherence to a procedure of pumping the tank for pressure and opening and closing valves at the correct time and temperature The Coleman stove is also prone to rust and spare parts are difficult to come by. Have a look at the Partner Steel range of cookers if you are interested in a stove which will last as long as you do. It is important therefore to carry large LPG canisters which will give you a couple of months cooking between refills. It is also very important to ensure that you have adaptors for different countries where refilling of tanks uses different connections. Filling a tank with butane instead of LPG can result in a month of weak flames and slow cooking dinners. If this happens it is important to empty and refill the tank with the correct fuel as soon as possible. Do not drive all the way from Argentina to Alaska while struggling to cook in wind and snow with a little blue flame no stronger than a lit fart.

Food Storage

Depending on the size of your vehicle and the number of passengers you carry you might want to invest in an electric cooler or a fridge. We swear by the Engel fridges but have also used a Waeco fridge for quite a few years. In fact we use both at the same time. The off-road fridges available are more expensive than the fridge you use in your home and draw the most electricity out of your vehicle. It is wise to consider installing solar panels on your vehicle to help generate the power for your fridge, though this is not completely necessary as one, or even two, fridges can be run efficiently off a secondary auxiliary battery provided that the state of cool in the fridge and the state of charge in the battery are maintained correctly. A fridge allows you to enjoy a cold beer and a steak at the end of a long day on the road, but is not ideal for the storage of most vegetables. Vegetables need to be stored in a well ventilated area and dry foods, spices, canned goods, peanut butter, etc should be stored in a dry foods crate. Here are a few tips for taking care of your fridge...

- Invest in an insulating cover for your fridge, the cover will help keep the exterior clean and the interior cool
- Ensure that the fridge fan is able to draw clean, fresh air
- The performance of the fridge will be dictated by the climate you are travelling through. Try to keep the fridge shaded and cool in hot temperatures
- To ensure optimal performance, do not open the fridge often or leave open for long periods of time. When cooking, remove all the ingredients you need, simultaneously and replace together
- Often a bag of ice or frozen bottle of water will help increase efficiency and reduce energy usage in hellishly hot locales
- The morning beer prep is essential. You want the beers to be ready when you are, after a long day on the road. Remember, putting hot items in the fridge will reduce efficiency so

be sure to put the cans in early in the morning when the cans are cool
- In order to preserve battery power levels, it may be necessary to turn the fridge off overnight. This is particularly true when camping for a few days without an electricity hook up or solar panels
- Run the fridge off a second, deep cycle "house" battery with a solenoid separating it from the vehicle battery to avoid starting issues
- Clean the fridge regularly and do not over fill. A chamois cloth left at the bottom of the fridge will absorb spills, excess moisture and leaks
- In cold climates, the fridge will usually operate very well.

Remember, again, where there are people there is food and as long as you have local currency you will be able to buy whatever you need. Unless you are planning to tour remote areas for an extended period of time, there is no need to buy bulk of anything. When we first travelled North of South Africa, we were told by the internet guru's that we needed large quantities of powdered milk, rice, flour, canned goods, meat etc, that we would not be able to buy any food or drink. Within a week we gave it all away and had a cheeseburger for dinner.

Washing and Cleaning Equipment

As stated previously it is advisable to carry a large square container for washing dishes and carrying water. Ideally this container should fit into another container or crate which should also contain...

- A pack of double sided washing sponges with the soft sponge section for general dish washing and a coarse side for scrubbing pots and pans. These types of sponges are suitable for non-stick cookware, as you do not want to use steel wool on non-stick surfaces
- A bottle of dishwashing liquid, bio-degradable if possible
- A set of dish cloths
- A set of cloths for cleaning the interior of the vehicle
- Dashboard spray, a quick daily clean of the interior of the vehicle makes each mornings departure more pleasant
- Small hand brush and pan to clean the interior of your vehicle and sleeping areas
- Laundry detergent and softener - liquid detergent is not recommended for hand washing.

Clothing

You might have noticed that we have an underwear fetish of sorts. We are serious about our undies. Each person in or on the vehicle should have twelve pairs of good quality, durable, comfortable under garments. The reason for this is simple. Laundry sucks. Unless you are in a truck with a built in washer/dryer, you will be spending a fair amount of time searching for a Laundromat or hunched over a basin scrubbing your delicates. A pair of shorts or trousers can be worn for a couple of weeks before needing a wash, while T-shirts may only last a few days depending on the climate. Jackets, hoodies and pullovers tend to need less frequent cleaning. Your under carriage should always be cool and dry, hygienically it is the correct thing to do.

There are a few very good outdoor clothing suppliers who have put a lot of time and energy into fabric technology. You don't really appreciate all the research and tech that goes into your outdoor clothing until you are wet in Patagonia. But when that clothing dries in mere minutes with only a gentle breeze and weak sunlight you begin to understand how this clothing is more than just talk and hype. The right clothing could potentially save your life if your adventures become mis-adventures. It is important to realise that you will also be able to buy clothing in most countries you are travelling to and will be able to buy a warm jacket or a pair of shoes if you need to. The challenge is to pack for the weather you will most likely encounter and any extremes such as high heat, high altitude and severe cold. Very large people may struggle to find clothing or shoes which will fit their gigantic frames.

In addition to the glut of underwear each person should have...

- 5 pairs of socks
- 3 pairs of trousers, the quick dry, multi pocketed, zip off legged ones are great. Bear in mind that if you wear the trousers as shorts and do not wash the zip off legs simultaneously the trousers will become two tone, the sign of a true long-termer
- 2 pairs of cargo shorts
- 2 pairs swimming trunks
- 8 T-shirts, any colour but white, preferably not with large marijuana leaf emblems
- A zip-able hoodie. The hoodie is great for travelling, you can zip it up when cold, open it up when warm and cover your head when you rob the bank to fund for your travels
- Hiking boots, comfortable loafers and a few pairs of flip flops. Remember to always wear your flip flops when showering in communal showers, this is the only effective way to prevent athletes foot.
- Spend the clever money on your shoes, bearing in mind that they will work extremely hard. I have a pair of Merrell's which have lasted six years, have been to Kilimanjaro, the Amazon and Alaska. Take care of your shoes and they will take care of you. A good bee wax waterproofing helps rejuvenate an old pair of kickers
- That comfortable wool beanie your Gran knitted
- A waterproof winter jacket with removable inner layer
- Dresses or skirts for the ladies or a few sarongs which can be transformed into both
- A Shemag scarf in dark colours. There are a few reasons to wear this scarf outdoors. Firstly, you look badass. Secondly, it is highly adaptable to any weather conditions. In extreme heat you can soak it in water and cover your head or neck for instant relief, in cold weather you can keep your neck and   face warm. It can also be used as an arm sling, a water filter, a bag, a towel and about fifty other uses. A damp Shemag will offer relief and help you sleep on the those hot, still evenings
- Honourable mentions:
  - Aqua shoes if you know you are going to spend a lot of time at the coast
  - Yoga pants for the fitties, a big no-no for the fatties
  - A speedo or G string if you are heading to Brazil, regardless of the size of your posterior, they really do not care
  - Mosquito repellent clothing for Africa, eventually the repellent wears off but the protection afforded in Malarial areas is priceless
  - Old clothing for wearing while working on your truck. Eventually all your clothing will be

old work clothing which will then be recycled into rags.

Remember to roll your clothes when packing, do not fold. Rolling tends to decrease the creases and compacts the clothing, thus taking up less space. Packing in bags is for lowly backpackers, if you have a rig, dedicate a drawer or a crate just for your clothing.

Laundry

Doing laundry sucks, let's be honest, but there is something strangely satisfying about a big pile of freshly washed and fragrant clothing. As a family of four, we have more than our fair share of laundry, Jessica will wear five outfits a day if she can get away with it, each outfit, worn once is automatically "dirty", and Keelan has a peculiar gift for getting clothing filthy as soon as he has put it on. I manage to cover all my clothing with either grease or food. We have over the years learnt a few time, energy and money saving laundry techniques...

1. The "wine stomp" is our preferred method. When arriving at a campsite you will usually decide within the first half hour whether you will be settled in for longer than a night. If so, grab your designated laundry crate, a large one if you're a family, and fill it with enough water to cover the clothing. Add your detergent and then step in, or get your iPod equipped 7 year old in there, and get stomping. Said stomping is to continue until your feet are wrinkled and your clothing is clean. Empty the crate of dirty water and replace with fresh water and a bit of softener. Repeat stomping, wring out clothing by hand and hang up to dry.
   - Carry a good length of nylon rope to string between trees (or from the vehicle roof rack to a pole, etc) as a washing line. A rope is always handy and we find it is better to have one piece of gear which can do many jobs rather than single purpose gear, such as a thin wash line.
   - Wooden clothes pegs are more durable than plastic.
2. Wash bucket with water tight lid - Place dirty clothing in the bucket with detergent and water and seal the lid before setting out for the day's drive. Upon arrival at the campsite your clothing would have gone through a decent wash cycle.
   There are several problems with this method (yes, we have tried this method a few times)...
   a) You may not find a suitable location at the end of the drive to dry the clothing
   b) The weather may change, ie, rain or very high winds or cold
   c) You may not find sufficient water available for rinsing the laundry
   d) If left in the bucket too long, the clothing may mold and will need to be washed again
   e) The lid may come off on very bad roads leading to a soggy mess
3. Wash bag - These are essentially dry bags with little knobbly bits inside. A great idea but not incredibly effective and if rubbing too vigorously may be too abrasive for your clothing
4. The washboard – old school AF. You might as well head down to the river and bang your laundry with a rock
5. Hand propelled washing machine similar to a large salad spinner
6. Mini washing machines – If you have a truck, then by all means, buy a machine that works – you might consider offering up the machine if you come across an overlander that has a small bundle of washing.

Of course, you will often be able to drop the laundry at a Laundromat which may or may not be quite expensive and may or may not actually clean your clothing. Some Laundromats will use the minimum detergent possible and, after a very short wash cycle, will toss the clothing in a dryer with some nice smelling stuff. Often clothing will be returned stained and shrunk.

After a few months of outdoor living, stomping and constant abuse; your clothing may lose much of its colour. Often dyeing clothing can revitalise it and give it a few more month's service. This represents quite a large saving for the budget conscious overlander.

Toiletries

Again, unless you plan on driving to Timbuktu, you will be able to find underarm products, soap, sanitary products for ladies and earbuds anywhere. Most toiletries last at least two months, therefore there is no need to pack in bulk. You will find that the more time you spend outdoors the less time you will spend looking at yourself in a mirror or needing to smell like a night club queue. Hygiene is far more important than a hairstyle. This may get gross...

- A few bars of soap. Anti-bacterial soap kills good and bad bacteria and you need both in equal quantities. Dove does not foam. Cheap, big bars of Lux or Palmolive do the trick
- Wet wipes. When you have been out there a few days without a shower, a good wipe of face, under carriage and arm pits is what you really need
- Hand sanitizer. We used to mock the Norwegians in Malawi every time they whipped out the hand sanitizer before meals. We had the trots, they never did. You want to shake hands with the friendly locals and you are going to be touching some pretty weird things. Before putting hand to mouth give your hands a quick wash with waterless hand sanitizer and clean with a wet wipe. Spending hours on the toilet because you ingested some local bug your body is not accustomed to is a recipe for misery. Be discreet when wiping your hands after greeting the locals, we do not want to give offence
- Nail clippers, 2 of, full size, stored in easy to reach places. Because you are spending most of your time outdoors you will want to keep your fingernails short and clean
- Earbuds are also good for cleaning car parts, actually
- Roll on anti-perspirant. No more using a quarter of a can of Blue Stratos every day before breakfast. Overlanders don't smell great, get used to it
- Toilet paper. It takes up plenty of space and weighs nothing. Use it to fill up empty areas in the rig which you don't want your significant other filling with crap. Keep it dry and two ply
- Body cream. In the desert and at high altitude you are going to crack up like a British high school teacher. Just not quite. Your skin will need hydrating and your lips will want to chap. Take care of your waterproof cover
- Toothpaste, 1 big tube
- Shampoo and conditioner, not 2 in 1. Short hair is the easiest to clean, style and maintain. If you insist on having long hair, plait it daily
- A good hair brush and a comb for your travel beard
- Pads and tampons. Pads can usually be used in case of emergency for large open wounds and used as an absorber when your Land Rover leaks constantly through the gaps in the doors during a storm
- Makeup is rarely needed, take as little as possible. A little bit of colour on the lips is usually

enough and unless you're planning to go partying at the local nightclub, you'll look like a fool walking around with makeup at a campsite, ladies, this applies to you too

- Eye drops. Take a few bottles as it needs to be kept in a cool dry place; and once opened, expires after a month
- Facial cream for them wrinkles. It is a common known fact amongst the older ladies that you accumulate a lot more wrinkles when exposed to the constant sun and extremes, make sure you have a good night and day cream
- Young ladies, take care of your tight porcelain skin. Long-term overlanding can be rough on a girl
- Birth control and/or hormone treatment – make sure you stock up if it's a specific brand or only available on script. Many countries allow you to buy these products over the counter and if you have a script, will allow you to purchase as much as you need
- Sunscreen. Don't read beauty magazines, they will only make you feel ugly. Wear sunscreen.

Recovery Gear

The further you get from the beaten track the more likely you are to encounter obstacles in the road. Being able to recover your vehicle without assistance is very important, especially if you are in a remote area with very little traffic of any sort. It is important to stress the difference between an off-roader and an overlander (more on that later). Overlanders do not go looking to get stuck but sometimes the road will throw sticky obstacles in your path. Recovery gear can be heavy and expensive and it is important for you to know what kind of long-term travelling you are going to be doing before you make the investment. Generally off-road recovery gear will include...

- A winch, rated to the weight of your vehicle
- A snatch block and tree protector
- A winch extension strap
- D shackles
- Leather gloves
- A snatch strap which uses another vehicle and kinetic energy to free a stuck vehicle
- A tow strap, which could be used to recover a vehicle and to tow a stricken vehicle to a safe repair point
- A short shovel
- Sand ladders
- A high lift jack with jacking plate (optional)
- Two blocks of wood
- An air compressor for the inflation of tyres and air jacks
- A stout wife.

An overlander who never intends to leave the paved road should rather spend the money saved on this gear on pedicures and peanut free products. I am kidding. Of course. Overlanders who intend to drive the Road of Bones in Russia and the BR319 in Brazil should carry most of the above gear. A personal preference, we do not carry a high lift jack, it is a heavy and dangerous piece of equipment which we have never missed. Others swear by the high lift jack and would not leave home without it.

Tiktaalik Field Knive Set by
Tools for Adventure

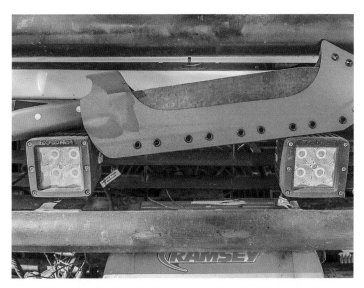

The Overland Machete by L.T.Wright
Handcrafted Knives

Universal propane tank adapter

Axes, Knives and Machetes

Machete's are, in our experience, more useful than axes. Used properly, a machete can cut through medium sized logs faster than most axes and is useful for rapid self defence. Essentially a machete is a sword which you get to carry legally in your vehicle through most border posts and can also be used for chopping wood or clearing overgrowth. When camping in remote areas and the paranoia sets in, you want your trusted machete close by your side. Hatchets are also very useful tools if used properly, whereas as a full size axe is really only useful if you know how to use it and you will be travelling through heavily wooded country for an extended period of time. If we had to choose between the full size axe and a machete we would choose the machete every time. Machetes are also light weight and easy to conceal. Ideally you want a machete which is about 60 centimetres long, with a 2mm thick spine, a sharp belly and edge and a decent, preferably leather, sheath. Hunting knives are not only really useful around camp but are also great for self-defense and will be your constant companion in the wild and when free camping, particularly if you are in a rooftop tent or a ground tent. It is worth mentioning that in our years overlanding we have never needed to defend ourselves, I do believe though that it is better to be prepared than caught off guard, particularly when you are responsible for the safety of a family, as I am.

By far the most useful bladed tool of them all is the trusty Leatherman. As a multi tool it is always close at hand, sitting on your hip. Minor repairs of gear and machine can often be done with one of the tools in the Leatherman's arsenal and the after sales service from the company is nothing short of excellent. The Leatherman pouch we have has a little pocket behind the blade which is perfect for storing a $100 bill in case of emergencies. But, by far, my favourite feature of the Wave version which I carry, are the two extremely sharp knife blades, one straight and the other with a wavy serration. I am always armed with a lethal weapon wherever I go and I can carry it in public places. People view it purely as a multi tool hanging from my belt but I know that if we are in a fight or flight situation and there exists no safe option for flight, that I can defend my family and property. And I can open a beer bottle after the duelling is done.

If you do choose to carry a full size axe, buy an American felling axe. For splitting logs, a splitting maul is the ideal tool but the felling axe is lighter and far more versatile. The heel of the blade extends down in a gentle arc providing protection for the inverse of the shaft shoulder where the shaft meets the axe head. Thanks to the current hipster obsession with all things lumberjack, there are a good few suppliers of beautiful, hand crafted axes. You could also walk into the nearest hardware store and buy an axe, they do the same job. Do not buy an axe from a 4x4 gear retailer before comparing prices. The axe can either be mounted on the vehicle or hidden away inside. We choose to mount the axe on the vehicle only when spending a significant amount of time in wood country. Driving in the desert with an axe hanging off the vehicle invites only mockery and derision.

An outdoorsman would not leave home without his Leatherman, machete and axe, then again, he knows exactly what he is going to do with each.

Miscellaneous

There is always going to be a pile of gadgets which you are never quite sure you will need and are never quite sure where to pack. There are also those items which you are always going to be looking for when you set up a long-term camp (by long-term we mean five days or more). We have a crate in our Land Rover dedicated to these miscellaneous items and it is the most accessible crate. Within this crate there is another, smaller crate which contains the little stuff you are always searching for. The contents include...

In the large crate
- Bottle jack
- Wheel spanner
- Cable ties
- Tent pegs
- Rubber mallet
- Tyre repair kit
- Bunjee chords and straps
- A small tool bag containing a few screwdrivers, long and short nose pliers, a small shifting spanner, 10mm, 13mm and 17mm spanners (because we drive a Land Rover).

The small crate contains
- Batteries
- Candles
- Sewing kit
- Super glue
- Small cable ties
- Fishing tackle
- Small snap flares
- Matches
- A bottle opener.

Digging for gear is my least favourite activity. I ask Luisa where something is, she will say "there". I will ask "where is there?" She will say "there!" I will ask, "where the hell is there!" "THERE, you idiot!". Always pack your gear in the same place every time, do not have five options for the storage of one thing. Store it "there" and leave it "there". The other golden rule of gear is that if you don't use it, lose it. Sell it on ebay, give it away, you will not miss it once it is gone. Generally, we work on a month of idle, if the kit has not been used in a month, it must go. This rule does not count for cold and hot weather gear or spares, tools and recovery gear.

Technology

The road kills technology. The combination of dust, heat, vibration, altitude and moisture will fizzle the motherboard and cook the hard drive of even the most hardy "travel" computer. Research which computers the military uses in the field and try and get your paws on a bit of that action, if you cannot, take precautions to protect your tech. Tablets and smartphones should be safely housed within protective cases, laptops and notebooks should also be stored safely in protective cases and snugly packed in a designated space in the vehicle while travelling. Most modern travellers travel with a combination, or all, of the following technology...

- Laptop or notebook
- Smartphone
- Tablet
- GPS (Global Positioning System)
- DSLR camera
- Small digital camera
- Action camera x 2, i.e. GoPro
- Voice recorder (popular with writers and bloggers)
- Satellite phone
- Binoculars
- Drone
- Kindle
- Chargers for each device
- Memory cards
- External hard drives.

The more passengers you have the more tech you will be carrying. These are also the devices which thieves are most interested in getting their filthy hands on. Just a quick look at the list should convince you that your rig should have a large, padded, lockable safe purely for the protection and transportation of this expensive equipment. Many photographers have learnt a very tough lesson – always remove memory cards from cameras after a "shoot". Thieves are not kind enough to remove the memory cards when they steal the camera and you could lose hundreds of your most treasured memories in one horrible burglary. When possible, store the memory cards and hard drives separate from the hardware perhaps in a little pocket by your sun visor or somewhere inconspicuous, process your photos regularly and up load your best images to the internet for safe keeping.

- Be sure to get travel insurance for all of your technology, including accidental damage insurance. You are almost guaranteed to have at least one claim within the first six months
- A little known fact is that technology is not a fan of high altitudes. Aeroplanes are pressurised, your rig is not and it is not a good idea for passengers to work on notebooks or devices while you are driving or camping at significant altitudes, which would be anything over 4000 metres (14 000 feet)
- Camera lenses must be protected from dust and dirt as they are very sensitive. A speck of dust on a lens can ruin an otherwise great photo. You can remove dust from lenses and the camera body by using your air compressor, if you have one. Alternatively you can buy a can of compressed air from a camera store if you happen to be in an area which has those facilities
- A GoPro camera is perfectly suited for the adventurous overlander lifestyle. The amount of accessories available can be a bit confusing but essentially you will probably use the vehicle mounts and the head mount most frequently. The sucker mount works fine on glass but should not be trusted on any other surface.

GEAR REVIEWS

I have never been a fan of electricity. It boggles my already struggling mind more than anything other than algebra or female psychology. Some might think it strange then that we have chosen to travel the planet in a Td5 Defender; a vehicle which was much maligned when first launched due to the inclusion of an engine control unit (ECU) whose life blood is electricity. Land Rover purists around the planet mourned the death of the simple, practical Defender. How could they ever trust a vehicle, which needed an IT technician to reboot a faulty computer or clear faults, to take them to the most remote corners of the globe. Initially we wanted to buy a 300Tdi 130 without ECU, but then found the Td5 at a reasonable price and decided to take the risk. So far we have not had any ECU problems, except for an easily remedied recurring engine cut outs, after a Land Rover technician failed to replug a sensor 5 years ago (touch wood).

There are two irreplaceable gadgets which we have learnt are worth far more than their retail value which significantly negate the risks of running a computer managed vehicle and which provide us peace of mind when far from civilization.

The Little Black Box

Manufactured in Johannesburg, South Africa by Innovative Auto, the Little Black Box (LBB) is my favourite gadget by a country mile, I adore this thing. I really learnt to love it when we were driving at around 5000 meters in the Peruvian Andes and the radiator cap failed to deal with those extreme pressures and vomited our precious coolant, repeatedly. If I had not installed the LBB (as advised by a Land Rover indie workshop in Cape Town), the engine would have overheated and I would have possibly destroyed my head gasket, or worse, and would have been stranded in the mountains with only very expensive options for recovery and repair. It is not impossible to conclude that without the LBB our journey through the Americas might have ended early. I find that most vehicles are equipped with unreliable sensors and, usually, by the time you notice the warning gauge the damage has been done.

The Little Black Box has the following features:

1. Coolant level sensor
   - A loss of coolant is often the first symptom of a mechanical failure, an alarm will sound when the coolant level drops below the minimum level sensors, allowing you to stop and repair before serious damage is done to the engine
   - Engine temperature sensor
   - A further fail safe, if the engine reaches an unsafe temperature an alarm will sound, giving you the opportunity to take action to prevent damage
2. Oil level sensor
3. Voltage level sensor
4. Alarm with mute option
   - The mute option is great when you are doing repairs and need to leave the ignition on
5. Start up component check sequence
   - The LBB will run through the sensors and check whether all levels are normal when you start the vehicle. This gives great peace of mind if you need to move quickly and have not had time to check the fluids etc.

The Innovative Auto website (www.littleblackbox.co.za) is about as high tech as a chocolate chip cookie but does have useful information such as DIY installation manuals, dealer directories and a calibration guide. Innovative Auto also provides a commercial version, which can limit speeds and auto shut down with failure, as well as other useful gizmos like a turbo timer, calibration tools and mini header tanks.
Retailing at only a few hundred dollars this is one bit of gear which is a no brainer, essentially it is a false economy not to have one.

No, we are not sponsored by Innovative Auto and we were not paid for this (or any) review. I have such a huge gratitude and respect for this product that I believe every vehicle owner should have this EMS (Engine Management System), or something similar, installed in every vehicle they own, not just the recreation rig.

Another South African company called Madman has a similar EMS (called the EMS1) which retails at around $230.00 (at time of writing) and includes features such as an Exhaust Gas Temperature sensor and is upgradable to allow a few more options. We have never used this product in our own vehicle but have heard good reports from those who use it.

Available at www.littleblackbox.co.za

The Nanocom

The Nanocom is a diagnostics tool, roughly the size of a small, fat calculator, which plugs directly into the Defenders ECU. The powers that be thought it unwise to invest in this gadget before we shipped the Landy across the Atlantic, the result being that when we absolutely had to buy it we had to add international bank charges, courier fees and an 80% customs duty to the purchase price. The moral of the story is, do not leave home without it, or similar, if you have a rig with an ECU.

The Nanocom allows an ordinary Joe to plug into his ECU and check for faults and then clear the faults, check the turbo boost, the coolant temperature, the cylinders, the voltage from the alternator and a host of other super nerdy, ultra-high tech things. A confident nerd could even remap the ECU using the Nanocom, I believe, which will alter the torque and power.

As I said before, electricity is not my friend, and I have not studied our Nanocom with the intention of making changes to the programming of the ECU. I would have to get a technician to help me do that and would never attempt to do any but basic tasks with the diagnostics tool. We have used the Nanocom as a diagnostics tool, to check for faults and fault codes which will detail system failures which will need repair. After the repair of any faults, we are then able to clear the fault codes. We have also used the tool to measure turbo boost and particularly coolant temperature.

When we had our radiator cap problem in the Andes, we were able to drive with the Nanocom plugged in after refilling the coolant tank. We could see the temperature of the coolant in real time. The temperature would slowly climb as we drove higher and higher, looking for the mountain pass which led down to a town in a valley. After every five kilometres the temperature would climb to 90, then 95, 98, 105, 110, and exactly at 112 the Little Black Box alarm would sound, announcing that the water had again flowed out, past the faulty water cap. Luisa would update me on the temperature of the coolant and I was allowed the luxury of being able to predict when the LBB alarm would sound and therefore could find a safe area to pull off that bloody, icy road and top up the coolant. We were starting to worry as the road verges were covered with thick folds of ice and we knew that the night time temperatures would be extreme, perhaps too extreme for our little family in a roof tent. A combination of the real time information digitally displayed on the Nanocom, the God awful Little Black Box alarm and some water sourced from a pool alongside the road we were able to drive up to the crest of the road. A few hundred metres from the summit the temperature reached 112 and the LBB screeched, I muted the alarm and continued to drive, up and then down, down, down. The LBB alarm light continued to flash but we could read on the Nanocom that the coolant temperature was dropping, from 112 down to 105, 98, 95, 90, 86 before eventually settling at 69. Not once during through the entire five-hour long debacle did the Defenders standard temperature gauge needle move past the middle of the arc towards red. Without a drop of water to spare to refill the header tank, we made it down to the town, called Chivay where we booked into a smelly little hostel and slept the sleep of the dead. In the morning we came up with a plan to relieve the pressure on that pathetic water cap by bypassing the thermostat, in

it's sealed housing, with plumbing pipes. The bush fix worked and escorted by my good friend Bill Rayner (a fellow Defender driver who found us wandering around Chivay and refused to continue to Cuzco before we permanently resolved our problem), we drove 200 km's back to the nearest city, all the while using the Nanocom to monitor the coolant temperature. The problem was resolved after a week long wait for a $5 replacement cap sent in from Lima.

Available at https://blackbox-solutions.com/

Portable Wireless Audio Speakers

Being a full time, long-term overlander is wonderful. Machetes, jerry cans, maps and sunburn are part of your everyday life. Most days are spent doing amazing things and almost every day on the road is an adventure. But even the roughest, toughest overlander will sometimes miss the simple luxuries of a home without wheels, of a couch and a remote control and a day with nothing to do but watch every movie in the Lord of The Rings saga, back to back. Chilling in your rig watching a movie or two on a laptop is fine, better if you are wearing earphones but if there are two of you (and you don't have a headphone audio splitter) the little microphone on your Mac is not going to do justice to the great battleground scenes or the deep, dark voice of Saruman. Neither will the speaker on your smart phone be up to the task when you are standing next to a fire, in the middle of nowhere, tanning some meat, swigging a beer and swaying to the beat. Using your rigs audio system when not driving is not advisable as you run the risk of running the battery dead and it already has so many other important jobs to do.

UE Boom

We love this speaker. The battery will last for days if used at low volume and it charges very quickly using the same cable connection as a Samsung Galaxy. Imagine that, a chargeable electronic device which shares a common port. The sound is so rich and deep it is difficult to imagine that it comes from such as small device (about 15cm tall with a 15cm circumference) and is perfect for both movies and music. They come in various colours and are so tough that even Mr. Roughntough overlander will struggle to break it. The only thing I do not like about the UE Boom is that is cylindrical and likes to roll around.

The Bose

The Bose is the Boss, but we prefer the UE Boom. The Bose is priced similarly, is not as pretty, the battery does not last as long, the squishy buttons are fiddly to work with, the sound is not as good and the Bose charges on a crappy plastic cradle which will not charge if not connected perfectly. That said the Bose is still a great speaker. Ok, maybe not great. It is a decent speaker. Which sucks.

The Marshall

If Bose is the Boss, the Marshall speaker is the King of Cool. So retro, so #Vanlife, so bloody good looking, the perfect compliment to your colour coded, surf board carrying, skate board equipped Westfalia. Much larger and more expensive than the other two speakers mentioned here, the Marshall is not as practical nor is the sound quality so much better as to negate the size or price. The girls will love it though, as you lie together after an epic session, she twirling her fingers in your beard, admiring your sad Jesus tattoo as you listen to Mumford and Sons, again.

Melvill and Moon Seat Covers

Melvill and Moon manufacture a broad range of high end handmade safari luggage, campaign furniture, canvas and leather safari accessories and safari-style seat covers. Their slogan is "Laudator temporis acti", essentially meaning "praiser of a time past".

People who play polo and eat at restaurants, my friends and I can barely afford, tend to make intelligent purchases. They buy clothes which last, vehicles which don't break, shoes which never lose their shine and wives who know how to suffer discretely. When the eventual divorce settlement is hammered out, the alimony agreed and one of the holiday homes handed over, the only items left on the table to be hotly contested are the children and the Melvill and Moon set. He surely cannot be expected to part with the campaign furniture and she simply must have the luggage. Truth be told she only needs the children because of the monthly maintenance payments and only wants the M&M luggage because he loves the set so dearly. I don't blame him for divorcing her.

You see, Melvill and Moon make products for men.

Men who effort effortlessly, men who seldom have manicured beards or beer bellies, never tattoos, and are as comfortable in the boardroom or bedroom as they are sailing a yacht or motivating an orange Defender across the Malaysian jungle to the tune of Carmina Burana, while chuckling at the lyrics. They are Old Spice men.

No Defender is complete without M&M seat covers. We have had our set for four years and they are yet to tear or even stain despite the constant abuse of a large sweaty family who travel to dirty places. Not one zip has broken or even a beautifully embossed metal button has come lose. The white canvas bag which the seat covers were delivered in has served as our laundry bag and not one thread has come unstitched, the printed logo almost as bright as the day we received it.

Next time you hear someone lament that, "they just don't make them like they used to" have him visit the nearest Melvill and Moon stockist. If he can't afford the product he simply does not understand value.

I think they should change their motto to "Clama Semel" (Cry Once).

Available at www.melvillandmoon.com

SnoMaster Fridge/Freezer

We have been travelling for a long time now. You might have noticed that I am a fat man who loves beer and my family consumes more meat than even the most carnivorous Uruguayan. What do beer and meat have in common? Well, they both need to be kept cold, or at the very least cool. We have always used two fridges while overlanding, an old, second hand 40L Engel and a shop bought 40L Waeco fridge, and have found both to have their strengths and weaknesses.

The Engel is reliable but power hungry and will drain your battery if left unsupervised. Naughty Engel.

The Waeco can be as temperamental as an aging drag queen, needing a solid 110 volt current or it will refuse to perform.

That said, both fridges worked their asses off trying to keep up with my thirst and operating under extreme demands of heat, cold and altitude. When we eventually retired the fridges, battered and beaten after almost five years of constant use, both were still working well, particularly when plugged into the American power grid, the Engel, however, refused to be powered by the Defenders battery and Engel USA were not even remotely interested in helping us revive the old girl.

We replaced both fridges with one Snomaster Classic Fridge/Freezer BD/C-60D. Immediately I liked the look of the fridge, I was amazed by the thickness of the insulating walls, I was not too impressed by the loose fitting fridge cover. I then plugged the fridge in and gave it a while to cool. This ambitious creature was cold in minutes! I lifted the top cage, placed a warm six pack at the bottom and within ten minutes was having a cold beer with my new best friend. I used my remote control to adjust and monitor the temperature of each of the two compartments. I had another beer. I was a happy man.

Those divider cages create compartments which only an overlander of the highest order could have designed. Gone are the squashed tomatoes and mystery meats lurking at the bottom of the fridge. Gone are the days of having to unpack and repack the fridge to get to a can, waiting down there where cold airs naturally goes. You can open the compartments individually. You can crack a beer using the Snomaster bottle opener attached to the side of the fridge. I am happy, but more importantly the wife is happy. Happy wife, happy life.

This fridge has had an easy life so far, it has only travelled two continents and has not yet travelled beaten, undulating third world roads. I don't doubt that she will be up to the task, though time will tell and I will tell you.

Available at www.snomasterusa.com

The Moka Pot

The moka pot, also known as a macchinetta (literally "small machine"), is a stove-top coffee maker that produces coffee by passing boiling water pressurized by steam through ground coffee. It was patented for the first time in Italy by the inventor Luigi De Ponti for Alfonso Bialetti, in 1933 and has become an iconic design, displayed in modern industrial art and design museums. We love it. Unfortunately we have the smaller version, which we found abandoned in a strange little campsite in Belize, which only makes one mug of coffee per boil. The moka pot is perfect for overlanding as it uses very little energy to boil, is robust, easy to clean and easy to pack. If you are a coffee lover you simply have to pack this pot and throw out the plunger or espresso maker or kettle and sieve combo. At around $35 US this pot is affordable and will not only travel the planet overland with you, it will also accompany your kids as they set off on their own adventures own day. If there is more than one coffee drinker in your rig, we suggest investing in a moka pot of appropriate proportions to avoid morning squabbles, hair pulling and other unpleasantries.

The Kermit Chair

I go through camping chairs like printer cartridges and I have no idea why. Actually, that is a lie. I am large, I sit a lot and I lean heavily on the right arm. My favourite activity is sitting in a camping chair, staring at a fire and throwing back a few cold ones. The chair has to bear my weight as I stand up and again when I plop back down. Because I have a large lap, I myself, make a good chair and my girls will often join me for a chat. The Oz Tent Jet chair was initially a good chair but it unfortunately did not stand the test of time and has suffered failures a more expensive pop rivet would have avoided, the Oz Tent King Kokoba chair was a superior product which lasted quite a few years.

Luisa had seen a set of chairs at the Snoverland Expo 2016 and she had set her sights on a set which we eventually received in January 2017. The chairs (and a small table) were hand made in Tennesee, they were called Kermit chairs and, Lordy, were they cute? We opened a tiny box and found four small oblong bags, each with a colour swatch attached to the canvas handles, two red and two blue. We looked at each other in disbelief. There was no way on earth that these tiny packages could contain chairs which could support a large child, let alone a large adult. We laughed, ahahaha, there must have been a mistake. Keelan assembled one chair, an activity which took a bit of concentration. The Kermit chairs are made from a combination of thin, varnished wood, small metal supports and canvas. He placed the little chair on the lawn and we all stood around it, doubtful, marveling at the little creature which sat before us, waiting to be sat on. "You first". "No way Jose, you first". I stepped my 130 kilogram body towards the little chair. It did not tremble. Slowly I sat, expecting to hear the splinter of devastated little wooden legs and to feel the lawn rise to smack my butt. Again, the little chair did not tremble. I rocked slowly, nothing. The chair mocked me, haha fat boy. I was comfortable, a bit low to the ground but comfortable nonetheless. In a matter of minutes Luisa and Keelan had assembled the three other chairs and the two little tables and soon we all sat in a semi circle, amazed, a tea party.

The Kermit chairs were not designed, they were engineered by someone who had probably just retired from NASA and who has a fascination with Japanese craft, feng shui and all things minimalist. His tiny but beautiful house is furnished with a Yoga mat, a spork, a EU Boom, a Leatherman, two sets of shoes, paper plates and a Kermit chair and table set. He (or she) designed the Kermit using the principles of torsion, trigonometry, alchemy and materials sourced from distant planets. My legs are just too long for the little Kermit chairs but, the good news, is that there is a larger variety, better suited to the larger variety of human, Luisa just placed the order for the wrong set. All things happen for a reason though and the set of four chairs and two tables all fit into the small storage box which I built under the Defender. The kids love their chairs and I love the sturdy tables which defy science to be strong and durable. I would not hesitate to recommend these chairs. Particularly to my fellow minimalists.

Avialable at www.kermitchair.com

Wacaco Minipresso

I am not a coffee connoisseur at all, a girlfriend introduced me to cappuccino when I was 19 and I had no idea how to add the three spoons of sugar. I know very little about cheese either, but that is a story for another time. Growing up we drank Ricoffy and when we were feeling larney we would have a cup of Frisco, mmm creamy (both Ricoffy and Frisco are South African, chicory heavy, instant coffee). As a kid I would watch those American movies where they would pour their coffee black from a glass jar and never lock their cars. I wondered why those cars were never stolen and why they did not add milk and sugar, though sometimes they apparently added cream. In Ecuador, a kind man gave us a bag of his finest coffee and I became hooked while writing We Will Be Free, without my daily fix I was a grumpy twat but then I discovered that hot, sweet coffee is dispensed, free, at gas stations in Colombia. Because our "on the road" routine is so varied, it is difficult to settle into a decent coffee routine. Usually I drink it if I remember to.

But, it was while we were converting our Defender into a live-in camper that I truly understood why Americans drink so much coffee. You see, intelligent people do these kinds of builds in fully equipped workshops, with plenty of time and readily available resources. We did the opposite and always had a deadline of some sort – a plane or ship to catch, the end of a housesitting gig, an overlander show in Germany. We worked ten, sometimes sixteen-hour days. We had to fabricate everything, Keelan (my son) and I trying to find solutions for complex problems using limited resources and tools. It was extremely hard work and sometimes we simply ran out of ideas and motivation. The following is an imagined advertising agency pitch I dreamed up some time after my coffee revelation.

Bearded, gruff and grey dad; ponytailed, blonde and tall son are working together on a Defender, fabricating a lock box for tools. Both are sitting on workshop stools, muscular, drop dead gorgeous, covered in denim and plaid and strategically placed grease, running out of ideas.

"Lets have some coffee, son".

Son uses a perfect hand to strike a dramatic match and light a retro gas stove. He places a picturesque kettle on the blue flame. Mumford and Sons plays in the background. The water boils, son uses the Wacaco coffee machine and a tanned muscular arm to pump out a couple espresso, dad sits manly sexy, out of focus in the background, deep in thought, Defender looking purposeful behind him. Son hands dad the coffee. Dad drinks, son drinks, damn, them boys are men! Dad begins to smile. "I've got it". Dad uses a plank of wood over sheet metal to hand bend the perfect tool box. The Doors, Break on Through plays on the radio. "Wacaco, coffee is inspiration".

No-one said it was a great pitch. But the story is true. When we were gassed and running out of ideas we would have a cup of coffee and the caffeine would reignite the brain resulting in ideas, this is why Americans have the best ideas, coffee truly is inspiration. Wacaco sent me a message on Instagram – "Hey, do you like coffee?". "No coffee imma grumpy bitch". I responded. The response seemed to confuse them a bit, it was late and I had not had any coffee. "Yes, I love coffee". They sent me a Wacaco Minipresso machine and, well, I fell in love. The machine, not much larger than a large handful, arrived in a zip-up hard case. You unscrew the top of the machine and fill a small filter cup with ground coffee and screw the top back on, then unscrew and fill the lower cup with hot water. Screw the cup back on, release the pump mechanism, flip the little machine and pump over the little espresso cup which clips on top of the lower cup. A few seconds later you have an inspiring, delicious little espresso. Boom. Day improves, ideas flow, shit gets done!

I am a Defender man, I appreciate practical design and built quality, I am also an overlander and I love any piece of gear which is light, compact, well-built and serves a purpose. My only gripe with the Nanopresso is that it is not KTM orange (the six detachable parts would be easier to locate in a cluttered camper if they were brightly coloured) and it delivers a relatively small espresso. That said, the Nanopresso is going with me wherever I go from now on, providing inspiration when this old brain has run out of the big ideas, big dreams demand.

Available at www.wacaco.com

Stanley Classic Vacuum Travel Coffee Press

Overlanding in the USA made me jealous. Almost every day we would camp surrounded by people in massive RV's, vehicles with granite counter tops, fake fireplaces and full bathrooms. Their comfort made me feel uncomfortable, squished with my family in a very large but relatively small rooftop tent. We would struggle to cook outside while the RV people would whip something up in their large kitchens before settling down in a plump leather chair to eat while watching a football match. I sat in an uncomfortable camping chair trying to gulp down my food, served on a plastic plate, before the wind blew all the heat out. When we left camp, I would cram my family into the Defender while the RV people would pilot those massive beasts from the comfort of a cockpit which included cup holders for both hands and feet, more plump leather chairs, climate control, stereo surround sound, a huge navigation system, bum warmers, lumbar support and cruise control. Wankers. My legs are heated by the gearbox, my seat has one position, my arm hangs out the window, my shoulder rubs the B pillar, my heater is broken, I have no cruise control, when it rains my feet get wet inside the vehicle and my right knee cramps so badly that I have to stop for a walk every fifteen meters.

I picture the RV people, barreling down the highway at 100 mph, listening to Seinfeld on the sound system while missus makes papa bear his fourteenth mug of fresh coffee. I eat my bottom lip to stay awake.

Luxury for me is a cold drink or, even better, a hot drink. We have gone through our fair share of flasks but have never found one which actually did what the label promised. Until Luisa found me a little gem. I must have been a very good boy because, one fine day, I was presented with a present. An all-in-one Stanley flask and coffee press. At first I thought it was just a flask but then Luisa boiled the kettle, poured some ground coffee, a tablespoon of honey and some milk into the flask before adding the hot water, stirring, waiting a minute, then using the Stanley press to extract the good stuff. She closed the lid and gave it to me. Hang on a second. She had just given me the equivalent of three mugs of coffee. I was sure it would be tepid within half an hour, it was not. Three hours later I still had hot coffee. Praise be!

This was luxury! To be able to drive down the highway, reach over and grab the flask, pop the top and slurp some delicious coffee elevated me. I now had 10% of the luxury those RV people enjoyed, but, I could still drive through the Amazon and over dunes and up the side of mountains, while staying awake. I was now a god.

Unfortunately, this story does not have a happy ending. We shipped the Land Rover from the USA to England and flew over to meet her. I clutched my Stanley press/flask every step of the way. While in the UK we found a housesitting gig, one of many.

A little square lady in blue welcomed us into her home and introduced us to an amazing little animal. His name is Paddy and he is the hero of this story, everyone else is a villain. Once we were convinced that the neighbor was the devil incarnate (that the neighbor was always watching and listening and would not hesitate to phone our little blue friend no matter where in the world she might be) and that little blue was born of pure blood and of incredible means we were given a tour of the house and property. It was suggested that one of our children might want to sleep in a shed with a bed at the end of the garden. We were instructed to walk little Paddy an hour a day and we were briefed extensively on the particular do's and don'ts. Not once were we told that her bedroom was off bounds, or that her coffee was grown, ground and sourced from a Colombian messiah, we were also not told that the house was held together with sticky tape and strategically place little nails which held everything from ornamental plates to shopping bags to towels. The house was so full of wonderful books that the building seemed to be sinking into the ground. One of the shelves, held together with sticky tape and small nails, eventually committed suicide shortly after we left and we were held accountable for murder.

Little Paddy was walked an hour every day and brushed every night, his teeth were brushed and we were sure to take care of the inflammation between his toes, caused by all that walking in the meadows. At night he lay next to me where I and my wife slept, upstairs in a loft made for small, blue people while my son slept in the spare room and my little daughter slept in the main bed. I slept with my hand on Paddy's ribs and he would not leave the house until I was ready to walk him in the morning, come rain or shine. I, being a villain, first had to have some Colombian Jesus coffee, of which there was plenty. I would fill my favorite Stanley flask and after walking Paddy and having a shower, using our soap, our shampoo and our conditioner, I then brushed my teeth with my toothbrush and, coincidentally, my own toothpaste, before settling down in a small chair made of balsa wood, by a small Thai girl with arthritis and a tube of paper glue, to work on our third book. An arm broke, we tried to fix it. For 25 days we ate our own food, using mostly our own pots and pans.

We kept the house clean even though housecleaners arrived every Monday to push a broom around. We were told not to wash the sheets as our little blue friend has them dry cleaned. The dryer broke and we were accused of its murder through negligence, a large glass water container cracked when my daughter filled it with hot water and an ornamental plate, regretfully, also broke. Our little blue friend arrived home an hour early on the last day, while we were packing and rushed us out the door, we told her about the broken water bottle and said we would replace it, "don't worry", she said, "breakages happen". We quickly took most our possessions and left the house in the condition we found it, albeit with less but still plenty coffee and a few of our possessions, including my beloved flask!. A day later we read a review which summed up our family as, "Just no, not with a barge pole, contact me for more information". What on earth did little blue think we were there for? We were house sitters for the love of, not once was it ever discussed that we would be engaging in any activities which required poles, large or small. I immediately phoned little blue who cheerfully asked me how I was. Strange. I asked about the review and she explained that she was tired and frustrated and that we had used all the coffee. I told her that we had already bought a replacement water container and that it would soon be delivered to her. I then asked, calmly and repeatedly, what we could do to rectify the situation with the words, "what do we need to replace or repair?". "No, no, it is fine" she said. "Ok then, will you consider changing your review, it will definitely not help when we apply for future assignments?" "Um, ok, bye bye". I thought that was that. She changed the review to "Just no, not with a barge pole". Wonderful. Over a few emails we were told that our possessions would be posted to us. They never arrived. When we enquired we were told that we should not go to her house or contact her again. Amicable, civil. We sent two new water containers, the first mysteriously disappeared and the second she refused to accept.

Among the list of grievous infractions were the following;

We left food in the food refuse bin. God forbid. When we put the bin out for collection we were told by the waste company that little blue had not paid the collection fee, we told little blue, she said ok. In hindsight perhaps we should have reheated the food and consumed it to spare our new friend inconvenience.

We left cardboard boxes in the waste area. When we arrived all of the waste bins were full after what could only have been a convention of little blues. Ugh. The boxes we left were flattened and neatly stored ready for collection. We used all the tea bags, toilet paper and salt. We used all the toilet paper (animals) and left dirty frying pans in the cupboard. Lies! Fabrication! If only we had spent some time doing a hand over when little blue returned then we could have addressed this litany of charges, but instead I am forced to try and convince you, dear reader, that we are clean and considerate people who have only had very good reviews and who have always gone above and beyond to ensure that all parties are satisfied (without the need for barge poles or other such phallic devices). It is all just too bloody frustrating and what kills me is that, when we were rushed out the door I left my beautiful Stanley coffee flask on the impeccably clean kitchen counter and it is now pressed to the livery lips of someone who does not deserve it. My only consolation is that the person who now uses it a true coffee connoisseur, someone who loves coffee so much that she would insult an innocent family and concoct a plan of character assassination in order to keep a very nice coffee flask, Bizarre.

In review: The flask was superb, the dog was outstanding, the house a nightmare, the owner an asshole and the neighbor lovely. Poor F ˙ ˙

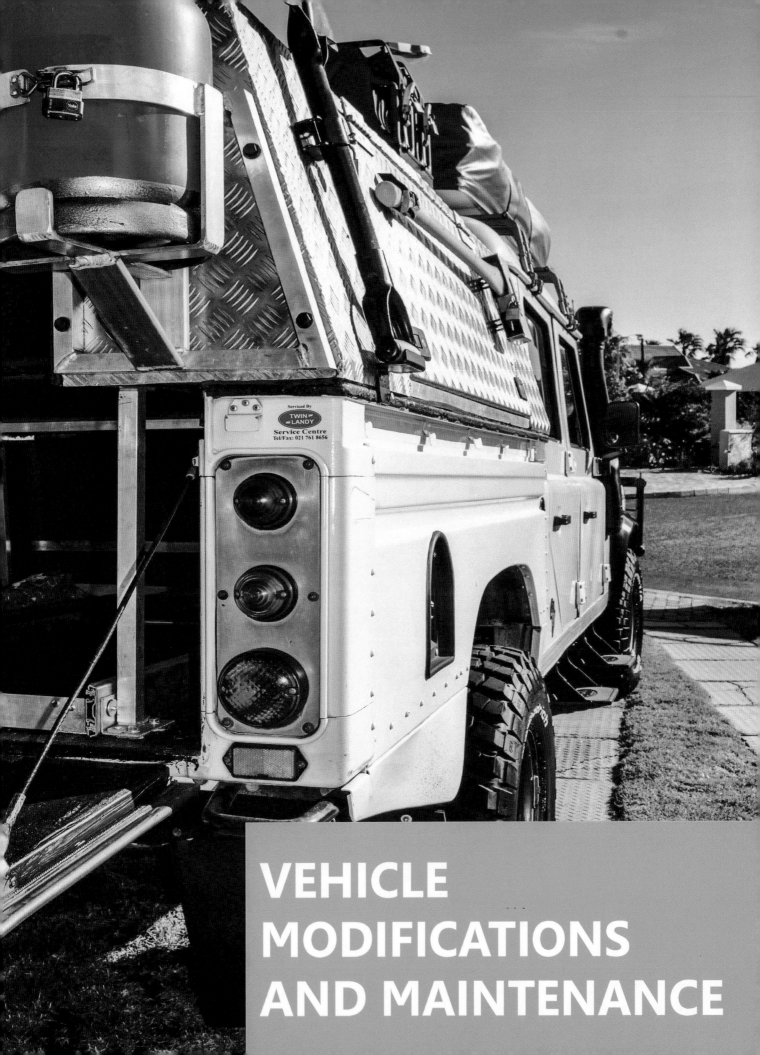

VEHICLE MODIFICATIONS AND MAINTENANCE

There is a very important distinction which needs to be made between the off-roader and the overland traveller; often the two are thought to be the same. An off-roader uses his vehicle, usually highly modified and not his daily driver, for recreational purposes and perhaps the odd holiday where he will venture into the realm of the overlander for a while. His priority is to test the limitations and endurance of both himself and his vehicle either in designated 4x4 areas or on a round trip to an adventure destination where he will rely on the vehicle to take him to remote places over difficult terrain. The off-roader has nerves of steel. The overlanders objective is adventure travel over vastly changing terrain while testing his own courage and resourcefulness and the vehicles endurance and reliability, all while maintaining some degree of comfort, usually over an extended period of time. Not all overlanders like to drive far from the beaten track and many will never exploit the off-road capabilities of their vehicles. There is nothing wrong with this way of travel. Many places we have been are accessible by a well driven, unloved sedan. If you are an off-roader who intends to become a long-term overlander you will have a fantastic journey if you are willing to adapt your mindset by carefully considering your long-term travel needs.

There is a European overlander I never met who toured central South America at the same time we were there (the first time around). We had mutual friends and the tales we heard were fresh. He drove a custom modified Pinzgauer based vehicle which resembled a lunar landing pod with wheels. The dashboard and ceiling of the drivers cab was equipped with knobs and dials and switches, lights that flashed and gauges to inform of the pressure, fluid level, heat and health of every bloody moving part. Antenna swayed above the vehicle and a satellite dish jutted out the side of the living quarters. He had upgraded almost every part and had installed an electrical system which would baffle most Electrical Engineers. The thing had six driven wheels, portal axles, lockers on each differential, self inflating tyres, you name it. It probably cost more than I have ever earned or spent, and I started working when I was 14. Problem was... the thing hardly ever worked. The electrical system would crash frequently and the highly tuned engine ate the gearbox and pooped out the clutch. Twice he had to have a technician and a huge crate of spare parts flown in from some spotless Swiss workshop. Those mechanical problems were undoubtedly an inconvenience and very, very frustrating, but we are going to assume that the overlander had a huge pile of Euros under his bed back home. The rub was that though the vehicle was designed to be highly competent off-road, it was unreliable and therefore unlikely to leave the hard top for any significant periods of time.

Contrary to popular belief, many overlanders are not able to afford either the over the top rig or the associated costs. If you are going to travel around the world in a 4x4, or any vehicle, you want to live by that old corporate chestnut. KISS, or Keep It Simple Silly. No doubt when planning to outfit your vehicle you will spend countless hours on the web and attending outdoor shows where gleaming hardware and camouflage strapping solar powered water filtration air beds will coax the hard earned cash right out of your pants. That burly, khaki clad salesman who once drove a fully kitted Toyota to REI, on a particularly wet and windy day, will convince you that you should not even consider leaving home without the rock sliders and the custom roof rack and the full length LED light bar, the three extra fuel and water tanks including the latest generation, NASA designed pumps installed by his workshop, while they drill in a cast iron drawer system, a full lighting system, a bar, two fridges, military grade under body protection, 40 inch tyres and all the associated upgrades to the running gear and electrical system. All of that is great if you plan to use the vehicle to impress your mates and a busty girl every second weekend, and once a year for a run to Moab or Morocco, but maybe not so great when you are planning to be a long-term traveller.

The focus when modifying a vehicle for overlanding should be on comfort and every day usability. You want to be dry when it is raining, warm when it is snowing or ice cold, cool in a heat wave, protected from the wind with the ability to store and prepare food under all those conditions and sleep well at night, safe from bugs and predators, both two and four legged. Recently we were camping in a desert with a leak of Defender drivers, a small sandstorm blew through camp all night. Everyone was miserable except for the genius who had put an ambulance body on his Defender and our family which could sleep in a tent through a tornado. Said genius (he really is a genius, a rock climbing PanAm vet who manages a team researching paediatric cancer), was warm and clean and safe behind insulated walls. He had sleeping space for two and could cook inside or outside the vehicle. He had one way blacked out windows for privacy, vents for ventilation and fans to cool the interior. The roof housed solar panels and surfboards, and had space for climbing gear or kayaks. Inside he had storage space for more than he needed and a large, lockable safe for cameras and other expensive technology as well as external storage boxes built into the ambulance body's cavities. I spent a day with him driving some low range routes in the surrounding mountains and was impressed that the Defenders off-road capabilities were not hindered at all. I was envious. The cherry on the cake was that he had spent the equivalent of the price of a new roof top tent on the conversion, but, being a genius, he had created that bit of luck.

Our advice to anyone planning a long-term overland journey is to first consider their particular style of travel and their own capabilities and requirements. If you like to get out there in the rough stuff and machete your way through a jungle, then you will need a vehicle equipped to be as tough as you are. If you prefer a gentle cruise with a bit of off piste driving and camping thrown in, then you will need a vehicle better suited to that style of travel. You will save a ton of money by investing in the vehicle which is best suited to your style of travel. How do you discover your style? Get out there and do it! Take whichever vehicle you have and go for a long drive, explore, meet other travellers and study their rigs. Only then will you know what is right for you.

Having read the last few chapters you should now have an idea of the type of vehicle which suits your travelling style and budget and you might have considered the gear and accessories which you will need to carry and accommodate on and in your vehicle. It is important that your vehicle is not overloaded with unnecessary weight.

What is GVM (or GVWR)?

"The gross vehicle weight rating (GVWR), or gross vehicle mass (GVM) is the maximum operating weight/mass of a vehicle as specified by the manufacturer including the vehicle's chassis, body, engine, engine fluids, fuel, accessories, driver, passengers and cargo but excluding that of any trailers". The GVWR limit for your vehicle can be found alongside other vehicle technical specifications on the Vehicle ID Plate which will usually be affixed to the inside edge of the driver's door or on the seat box. Here is an example of the Vehicle ID plate on an older model Land Rover.

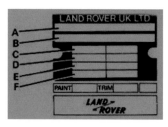

A= type approval
B=VIN (minimum of 17 digits)
C= max load weight permitted
D= max vehicle & trailer weight
E= max road weight front axle
F= max road weight rear axle

C = max load weight permitted is the GVM of the vehicle and this is the figure which interests us the most. For instance, our Defender 130, Double Cab has a Curb Weight or Tare (T), the standard weight of the vehicle without a load, of 2086 kg's. She is big and beautiful and mostly built of aluminium. The BVM is 3500 kg's. This means that we are able to carry 1414 kg's of passengers, accessories, gear and general crap.

During the development phase, manufacturers will test the vehicle's operation under load and will establish a GVM based on the performance of the vehicle and, one must assume, the limit of safe operation under load. Anyone who has travelled to a developing nation will understand that drivers are often quite happy to load the vehicle according to space available with total disregard to the GVM, if they are even aware that such a thing exists. It is not completely unreasonable to imagine that the official GVM of any vehicle is in fact understated as the manufacturers and dealers do not want to run the risk of warranty and fault claims which could arise if vehicles are proven to fail under large loads. You should, however, regard the GVM as the goal limit of your vehicles load carrying capabilities and plan the modification and load of the vehicle accordingly.

It is very easy to overload an overland vehicle, be it a bicycle, a van, a 4x4 or a truck. Imagine that you are driving a 4x4 and you have installed...

- spare fuel tank - 100 kg's when full
- two spare tyres and rims weighing 80 kg's
- a high lift jack weighing 20 kg's
- a roof top tent weighing 70 kg's
- four Jerry cans (two water, two fuel) weighing 100 kg's full
- a roof rack of 50 kg's
- a water tank full at 100 kg's
- a 100 kg drawer system
- an extra battery of 20 kg's
- a 9500 lbs winch weighing 50 kg's
- four occupants weighing a total of 300 kg's

That is already 990 kg's of extra weight before we have added spare parts, fridges, clothes, food, beer, first aid kit, recovery kit, technology, cooking equipment, LPG tanks, etc. If I am going to stay within the GVM of the vehicle I am going to have to lose some weight, both on the vehicle and around my waist.

The above scenario is one of the reasons that an overlander 4x4 vehicle should not be equipped as you would a normal, hard working 4x4. Here are a few tips for reducing weight...

- use load bars to support the roof top tent instead of an expensive roof rack
- carry only one spare tyre on rim
- carry extra fuel in one Jerry can and fill the spare fuel tank and Jerry can with fuel only when necessary
- replace the steel winch cable with a lighter, stronger synthetic cable
- ditch the high lift jack, unless you are a hardcore off-roader and you are accustomed to using the high lift
- install a light weight drawer system
- use aluminium accessories where possible
- live by the golden rule, if you don't use it – lose it. If you have not used a particular piece of gear for over a month and it is part of your daily used articles, such as
- cooking equipment, sell it or give it away
- forego the heavy and expensive rock sliders, aftermarket bumpers, bull bars and full underbody protection if you do not intend to go looking for the rough stuff go on a diet. Easier said than done.

Your vehicle carries two types of weight, sprung and un-sprung weight. Basically, sprung weight is the weight above the suspension (from the chassis up) and un-sprung is the weight underneath the suspension (the axles, tyres and rims, propshafts). There is not much that you can do to alter the unsprung weight (with the exception of installing aftermarket tyres and rims), it is the sprung weight which is of greater concern.

There are ways to increase the load carrying capacity of your vehicle (your GVM can not be changed at all unless officially by the manufacturer):
- install heavy duty steel rims with a load bearing tyre, i.e load range E (more on that later)
- upgrade the suspension of your vehicle whether coil or leaf sprung
- install air bags in the rear suspension
- load the vehicle evenly, concentrate weight low
- reinforce the chassis, particularly the rear overhang section behind the rear wheels

* Remember to adjust your headlights. A vehicle, heavily loaded in the rear, will drive "nose up" and your headlights will need to be adjusted down. If your vehicle is suffering from excessive "nose up" it might be time to consider dumping some gear and upgrading the rear suspension.

Tyres

There are many schools of thought when it comes to the perfect tyre. Well, as with overland vehicles, there is no perfect tyre. We learnt the hard way, that running the correct wheel/tyre combo before leaving home can save you a lot of money, pain and suffering. You want to be able to trust your tyres and suffer as few punctures as possible. Rubber technology is not what it used to be and those original vehicle based explorers were running terribly overloaded vehicles on horrible pieces of rubber. The technology in today's tyres is simply astounding and a good set of tyres could last you 80 000 km's if not more. In my opinion the perfect size tyre for my Land Rover is a 285/75 R16 All Terrain. This tyre will have a load range E which is equivalent to 1700 kg's per tyre. It is tall enough to raise the vehicle differentials 3 cm's higher than standard and wide enough to provide excellent traction in mud and sand. The

Defender 130 is a bit of a sausage dog on the factory equipped tyres and a taller, wider tyre on offset rims reduces body roll, improves the vehicles stance and looks kick ass. Aesthetics are important to some and completely irrelevant to others, we love looking at our truck and so do others, she is a beauty.

Most overlanding is done on paved roads, how much time you spend off-road is almost entirely up to you. A mud terrain tyre, or MT, offers excellent off-road grip and traction in most off-road situations but can be noisy on paved roads and may not cope as well as other tyres in wet conditions and in the snow. An all terrain tyre, or AT, is better suited to a variety of terrains but will be less effective than an MT tyre in sand and mud and other off-road applications. With experience you will decide which tyre is best suited to your travel, style and vehicle. A wise decision may be to run the tyres as specified by the manufacturer, or as close to the size specified as changing tyre sizes may have various influences on the vehicles performance and mechanics...

- Wider tyres tend to put more strain on wheels bearings
- A taller tyre may raise the centre of gravity and influence the speedometer reading
- Larger tyres are heavier than standard sizes
- Larger tyres raise fuel consumption and road noise
- Larger tyres are generally more expensive.

My own personal preference contradicts most of the advice I have just given you. I have run 33/12.5 R15 Mud Terrain tyres with a load range C for the last 70 000 km's (one set) and before that I ran a set of 32/11.5 R 15's for 75 000 km's. Yes, I did initially have problems with wheel bearings but otherwise the tyres have performed admirably and have not damaged my vehicle mechanically. I chose to put the 33's on in Colombia after we made the decision to drive back to Brazil through sections of the Amazon, in the rainy season. I know other overlanders, Engineers and others far more intelligent than I, who run the same size tyres on heavier vehicles. I justify my choice of tyre by saying, "well, if they're good enough for them then they're good enough for me". The only major drawback of the wide MT's is that they protrude past the wheel arches and fling poo and mud all over my arm and the vehicle when we are in the shitty stuff. The Landy looks great, all covered in mud, but the wife is not happy with a dirty home.

By rotating and aligning your wheels and tyres often and maintaining the correct air pressures you should be able to get very good life out of a set of modern tyres. I know a Norwegian who drove a Nissan Patrol with 37 inch tyres from Alaska to Argentina then shipped to South Africa and drove back up to Norway without ever having a puncture or changing tyres. For the proper care and maintenance of your tyres you should carry....

1. A repair kit which consists of sticky plugs and the plugging tool
2. A reliable tyre pressure gauge
3. A valve key for the quick deflation of tyres
4. Spare valves
5. A compressor, powerful enough to inflate the tyres on your fully loaded rig. If possible the compressor should be built into the engine bay or other concealed area of your rig. This

compressor can also run air tools if powerful enough and if you are planning to do your own mechanical repairs.

Take some time to study and understand the information and codes which are embossed on the sidewalls of your tyres. Ask your local tyre fitment centre to explain the information on your tyres and spend a while researching that information on the internet. You will need to pay particular attention to the max load tyre pressures and ensure that you are running your tyres at the correct pressure as driving for long periods with incorrectly inflated tyres will cause premature wear and can have a significant impact on your average fuel consumption. Be sure to check the date of manufacture on the tyre before purchasing, as an older tyre will degrade faster than a newer tyre.

Comfort vs Necessity

Comfort is relative. Some simply cannot live without a microwave oven and a TV, others are happy with a warm bed and a great view. Generally, more comfort equates to spending more cash. If you are a Cyclist or a Biker, forget about comfort. You will be sleeping rough and living hard, which may just be the best way to live. You will appreciate a soft bed and a snooze in a hammock more than anyone other than a walker, but then again a walker wants to suffer, that's why they walk. Roof top tenters have a lovely nest to live in but are still in a tent, no matter how much it costs. Motorhomers and Truckers have the most comfort but the least mobility, it is all a trade off. Comfort weighs a lot. Earlier we mentioned that you want to be, "dry when it is raining, warm when it is snowing or ice cold,/cool in a heat wave, protected from the wind with the ability to store and prepare food under all those conditions and sleep well at night, safe from bugs and predators, both two and four legged". If you are going to build a rig, either by hand or by commission, you will want to take that sentence seriously, keeping in mind the constraints of budget, space, weight and mobility. There is no sense spending all your money building your perfect rig and having no cash left for travel. Here are some tips to help you save money when outfitting an overland vehicle...

- Do it yourself. If you have the skill, motivation and time, you can put together a great rig at a fraction of the cost to have it built, or
- Find an outfitter who is an overlander with a good reputation. They will understand your needs come before their immediate profit and will help you put together a rig which suits you and your budget
- Being able to sleep inside your vehicle inconspicuously will save you a lot of money in the future as you will be able to safely free camp in many areas, including cities
- Do not waste money on gizmos and gadgets, camp as often as you can and test your set up, find what is sorely lacking, borrow different gear to test or, if you live in the USA, buy stuff from REI and return it if it does not work for you. Invest in quality when you do eventually buy for the long-term
- Check your ego. It does not have to be the biggest or the flashiest or the most technically advanced machine on the road. The good people you meet will not care if you are in a VW Beetle or a Pinzgauer, as long as you do not suck as a person
- Understand which aspects of overlanding will satisfy you the most, and equip yourself accordingly
- Try and predict the future. The future overlander you is going to be a different creature to the you today, try and imagine what is important and necessary for the happiness of the future you. I will give you a tip. Future you, wants present you to save money, to spend way less money on crap, to toughen up and camp from day one. Future you, wants you to get by on as little as possible today so that he can keep on exploring the world. Future you also wants you to build a rig that will be comfortable enough for him to live in every day, built with taste and intelligence and moderation
- Spend less on complicated pump driven water filtration systems and a bit more on solar power and an energy grid which will not leave you powerless or stranded
- Fly and buy. Many overlanders buy a vehicle, drive it across the continent then sell it to the next overlander who does the same in reverse. You will not need to outfit or ship the vehicle and you should get most of your money back when you sell it, if you have not bought a lemon. You can, for instance, pick up an old camper in the USA for peanuts then drive it down to South America.

Trailers

Trailers are loved by some and loathed by others and are worth investigating diligently, as a new off-road trailer (equipped with roof top tent and drawer systems, awning) etc. can cost more than a second hand 4x4. Of course you could just tow a small trailer behind your Ford Fiesta, again, it all depends on your own budget, requirements and style of travel.

One of the drawbacks of overlanding with a roof top tent on your vehicle is that, once set up in a camp, it takes a while to close everything up before heading out to explore or even just for a supply run. There are stand alone frames which can be attached to the tent and allows it to stand independently but I have never seen this system being used on the road. A trailer with roof top tent mounted is a great solution. Essentially you are able to set up camp independent of the vehicle which allows greater mobility. The trailer also allows greater load capability which can be both an advantage and a disadvantage. A couple travelling in a Land Rover Defender 90 (Sirocco Overland) drove across Europe and Russia towing an off-road trailer. Anyone who has ever owned or travelled in a 90 will understand that, while the vehicle is fantastically capable, the storage space leaves a lot to be desired. Interestingly, we met a French couple in Peru also driving a 90. They did not have a trailer but had all their gear stored in round waterproof storage kegs, the kind they use on boats. At night they would arrange a platform on top of the kegs and over the front seats and that was where they slept. The man was not small but somehow they managed to sleep in that tiny claustrophobic space. I would rather have a trailer, a roof top tent or even a ground tent.

A South African family, (the Visser's) once drove from South Africa to Europe up the East Coast of Africa then back home along the West Coast after touring Europe. Many "experts" told them that it was a mistake to take a trailer but they completed the journey with very few problems. The tow vehicle was a Toyota Land Cruiser 100 Series and the children were both very young.

We have often considered investing in a trailer. In my dreams I picture a sturdy off-road trailer with an axle equal in width to the Defenders and with matching tyres. I picture a KTM parked in the middle of the trailer with a drawer system on either side, a kayak strapped to either side of an external frame which supports a roof top tent, Jerry cans and LPG canisters on the nose for weight and a couple of bicycles hanging off the back. The drawer systems will contain all our tools and spare parts and kitchen stuff. Perhaps one day.

The pros and cons of having a trailer:

Pros:
- Greater load carrying capability
- The ability to set up camp independent of the vehicle
- Extra spare tyres (if the trailer uses the same tyres as the tow vehicle)
- The ability to carry "toys" such as bicycles and kayaks
- The ability to carry more provisions such as fuel, LPG, food and water
- For larger families a roof tent on a trailer and a roof tent on the vehicle will provide sufficient sleeping area and privacy
- Both vehicles are independent of each and can be bought, sold or repaired individually

Cons:
- Cost of the trailer
- The weight of a fully loaded trailer and the resulting strain on the tow vehicle
- The trailer limits technical off-road capability
- More tyres to wear down and replace
- Risk of failure, the more stuff you have the more there is to go wrong

-   Reversing and parking can be difficult.

There are a few South African manufacturers of off-road trailers of very high quality. Given the exchange rate of the Rand to the major currencies (and the low probability of economic improvement), it would be a great idea for anyone looking to travel the world overland with a trailer, to buy both the trailer and vehicle in South Africa and then begin their journey from there. There are also excellent overland outfitters and the standard of workmanship is generally very high.

Image credit Sirocco Overland

The Roof Top Tent (RTT)

By installing a RTT any vehicle instantly becomes a home. There are no major modifications which need to be done to the vehicle other than the installation of load bars or a roof rack. A RTT also does not hinder the vehicles off-road capability significantly. We have only ever overlanded with a RTT and we are a family of four, we love our Howling Moon RTT and it only seems fair that we acknowledge how indestructible their product is. Our first weekend overlanding in South America we were hit by a cyclone and were stuck in the tent for three days while the wind howled and the rain pelted. With the annex attached we had a decent space to spend the days playing cards, cooking and waiting out the storm. The tent itself did not leak despite the constant assault of the cyclone and it was only when the trees in the forest next to our camp started to fall that we decided it was time to find safer lodging. That is one tough tent. We spent 80% of the next three years sleeping in the tent and it is good for at least another three years partly because of it's excellent construction and partly because we coated every inch and seam with plenty of Scotchguard canvas sealer when we first received the tent. The weakest parts of any RTT are the rain fly, the zips and mosquito netting, it may be a good idea to carry spares if you intend to travel for long periods.

1. Be 6'5". Short people really struggle with a RTT especially if it is perched on top of a tall vehicle
2. If you have a travel companion work as a team to open and close the tent
3. When opening the tent, roll up the cover and wedge it under the base of the tent, you can install special straps to hold it in place. By rolling the cover up and keeping it out of the way you will protect it from the elements and reduce your frustration while trying to access whichever door or window the cover may block
4. You will want to ensure that the vehicle is parked on a level surface so as to avoid a slow roll out the tent at night. Carry either plastic levelling blocks or a couple of blocks of wood for this purpose
5. Tie a plastic bag to the ladder for your shoes or fabricate a pull out step like our friend, Bill Soucess
6. The midnight/early morning pee can be a real pain when sleeping in a RTT. One solution is to keep a designated pee bottle in the tent. The other is to attach a funnel to a length of hose which runs out of the tent into a bottle on the ground. If you ever see someone using the funnel/hose/bottle DO NOT clamp the hose. That WILL NOT be an extremely funny prank
7. For lighting you can install LED lights in the tent with minimal fuss or you could use solar lamps as using a head torch every night will become expensive. Try to use lamps with a soft glow
8. Ditch the sleeping bags and inflatable pillows and use down duvets and pillows, you will be so much more comfortable. When closing the tent, fold the bedding into the half of the RTT above the vehicle and compress as much as possible, being sure to not let the bedding interfere with the tent poles when closing
9. Throw away the horrible Velcro straps that come with the tent and attach a couple of ratchets with corresponding straps
10. If possible have the manufacturer install two large YKK zips on the tent cover, this way you can easily zip from two directions and if the one zip breaks you will still be able to use the other for the complete zip-able area
11. When closing the tent have one person tuck the tent fabric in while the other lifts and lowers the other half of the tent using the ladder for easy leverage
12. Flip the cover over and pull firmly over the edges of the tent, then throw the ratchet straps over (weighted with a tin cup or similar if the wind is blowing) and then ratchet the tent closed
13. By using the ratchets you will be able to compress the bedding inside the tent and therefore be able to zip the tent closed with much less effort
14. If the wind is being uncooperative, move the vehicle (with the tent open and the ladders lifted) so that the wind works in your favour
15. Be sure to relieve some of the tension in the ratchets once the tent is completely zipped. Over time the ratchet straps will damage the tent cover, it may be a good idea to glue or stitch some extra material over the rubbing points
16. Count the window pegs before putting them away
17. Regularly lubricate the tent ladders and zips.

Dealing with damp

There will be those days when you get caught by bad weather. You have two options when touring with a RTT, either wait out the weather or try to drive towards better weather. If it is raining or snowing for a week in all directions you may have to wait it out. Many mornings the tent will be covered in dew and you will need to wait for the sun and wind to dry the tent. We had a revelation the other day... We have always been early morning people but since we started travelling long-term we have begun to get out of bed late in the mornings, sometimes only showing our faces after 9 am. Initially I thought we were just becoming lazy overlanders but then I realised that the reason we began sleeping late in the first place was because we were waiting for the tent to dry after the morning dew or night rain. What else do you do in a tent but have a snooze while waiting for the sun to rise and dry the tent? That is my excuse and I am sticking to it. Usually the tent will dry while you go about your morning routine.

⏏ If rain is persistent and you need to get on the road, wait for a break in the deluge then use a towel in need of washing to dry the tent as best you can before closing it

⏏ Try to close the tent only when it is dry and open the tent as soon as possible if it was closed wet. The dampness will destroy the tent and bedding if left closed when damp for a significant period of time

⏏ Condensation in the tent can lead to a special type of water torture as drips form on the inside of the tent, roll down the canvas and drop into your sleeping face or eye or ear. To combat the condensation, we installed two highly absorbent Peruvian sheets of colourful Alpaca wool over the interior support poles of the tent. The sheets not only absorb the moisture but also give the tent a less militant, more homely feel

To avoid condensation under the mattress, try and get hold of an anti-condensation mat or individual pods. We clean out our entire tent on a weekly basis when doing the linen, where we aerate the mattress and if possible, hose down the entire tent

Taking care of your roof tent will ensure that it will last for many years and, with time, there will probably be nowhere else where you would rather lay your head

When you are finally finished building your rig and before you leave home permanently, go camping for a week test all of your gear and decide what should stay in the vehicle and what should be left behind.

Blending In Or Standing Out

While free camping one day, a medium sized furniture delivery truck pulled up next to our Landy. The trucks rectangular load pod had no windows at all, but had the large logo of a removal company on both sides and the rear, and two young Germans in the cab. When they opened the back of the vehicle we were surprised to see they could stand upright inside and had only a couple of cots, a camping fridge and a bunch of camping and hiking gear. They were travelling completely incognito. Standing side by side, the two overland vehicles were in stark contrast to one another. Our Landy, with the awning, shovel, roof top tent and Jerry cans and all the other overlander paraphernalia, was clearly a travelling vehicle which stood out like a sore thumb, everywhere she went people would take photos and videos of her. The Germans were invisible. They could drive down any highway or through any city and no one would turn their heads. They could park in loading zones and even make some extra money delivering furniture if they ran out of cash. The van had sufficient ground clearance for rutted dirt roads and a high load capacity. We could see the advantages of travelling in such a vehicle.

We have come across other overland vehicles covered in flags and stickers or huge maps with routes drawn on them and huge nationality stickers, the drivers name and nationality on the drivers door and the same for the passenger on their door. The sponsored travellers will have bright corporate branding, website and blog addresses clearly visible. These overlanders want to attract attention to themselves for whatever reason.

I will admit that when we started out, we too had stickers and logos plastered all over the Landy. We were mimicking high profile expeditions and were eager to take a million photos and reams of video which would be splashed all over the internet, attracting corporations and perhaps a large social media following. Within a few months we removed most of the stickers. We took a look at other long-term travellers and realised that they might have a few small flags on the vehicle but not much else in terms of self-promotion. We felt like we were bragging a bit and found that we were far more comfortable being less conspicuous, choosing rather to direct people to our website where they could take their time to enjoy our photos and read the raving reviews of our gear sponsors, if and when they chose to. If you are setting a new world record and raising a million bucks for charity, feel free to shine like the sun. Otherwise our advice would be to keep the branding and unnecessary adornment to a minimum.

When we asked the German boys in the furniture truck what motivated them to travel incognito, their answer did not surprise us. They were almost purely motivated by security concerns. Perhaps mom and dad had insisted that they would only hand over the Euro's if our young friends promised to take extraordinary steps to stay safe. Did we mention that they were touring only the USA. Their truck would have been a great long-term overland vehicle if they had installed a few big windows, painted the whole rig khaki and attached an awning. Travelling like a FBI surveillance crew is completely unnecessary, but the choice is yours how visible you want to be.

Maintenance

You might be one of those overlanders who never gets their hands dirty, who does not know how to change the oil in your rig or even how to change a tyre. Believe me, you don't want to be that guy. There is a wonderful sense of self sufficiency and comfort that can be had by taking care of your own vehicle. Understanding mechanical basics is not too difficult, you are an intelligent person after all, if not you would not be an overlander. Being able to take care of mechanical problems will save you a huge amount of time and money and may be the difference between life and death in some extreme circumstances. You owe it to yourself and your loved ones to make an effort to keep your rig running as it should be. Here are ten tips. You can thank us later, maybe a cold beer in a camp sometime...

1. Prevention is infinitely superior to cure. Get to know your truck before you leave, identify common faults with your type of vehicle and either pre-repair or prepare for those failures by carrying the relevant spares and repair manuals
2. Don't be lazy. It is easy to ignore that wobble or grinding or leaking when you are in a nice sunny camp with a cold beer beckoning and a welcoming hammock swaying in the breeze. Start with a small job and work your way to the bigger jobs, overlander vehicles take a beating and there is always something that needs a bit of TLC. Start with the squeak and work your way up to the wobble or grind
3. Lube, lube, lube. Metallic auto parts get hot and when they overheat they lose structural integrity resulting in failures and breakdowns. Oil and oil filters must be checked and changed regularly and religiously. Prop shafts must be greased with every service, wheel bearings checked, swivel grease and differentials topped up. Use the highest quality oil and lubrication you can source and afford and try to adhere to the manufacturer's specifications. Take care of your chassis. Give it a good high pressure wash once a month then coat it with a good thick spray of lubricant. You can use old engine oil or WD40. The chassis is the spine of your beloved truck's body, take care of it and it will take care of you
4. Stop, drop and roll. When the inevitable breakdown sneaks up on you half way up a mountain as the sun is setting in the middle of bloody nowhere, you will need to remain calm, assess the situation and do your best to get the wheels rolling again without the help of mechanics and tow trucks. Don't scream out expletives, don't pound the steering wheel and do not kick a rock and break your toe. These things are not helpful
5. Memorise the road features as you travel. You will not always know what lies on the road ahead but you do know what lies behind you. A truck stop, emergency parking area, shady tree or farmhouse can offer a safe, secure place to return to, to do your running repairs
6. The mighty Internet is your greatest resource. Find an internet connection and log onto a

forum which is vehicle specific. There are an equal number of gurus and orangutans out there dishing out pearls of knowledge and steaming piles of dung, you need to sift through the one true democracy to find your solution. Search for parts, arrange a courier or find a fellow traveller headed your way, transfer money and upload a bunch of breakdown photos to your blog. Your followers, friends and family love you and admire your travels and wonderful photos but what they really want to see is you up to your neck in grease, covered in red ants, in a muddy hole with a chunk of twisted metal in your paws. That will teach you for being a tough guy, tough guy

7. Carry a good range of spares and tools including special, vehicle specific tools and be prepared to be creative. I once had to change a fan bearing in Tupiza, a little city in Bolivia which had twenty small hardware stores but No 12 Allen keys. I had the special fan tool to remove the fan but found out that I needed two special tools not just the one. Under a searing high altitude sun, I ripped the skin off my knuckles trying to get purchase with an improvised tool made out of two spanners, nuts, bolts and duct tape. Eventually I succeeded. Little ratcheting spanners will save you hours of frustration and, if you drive a Landy, try to carry extra 10's, 13's, 15's and 17's. There are two types of spares – service and repair. Service includes all regular service items, filters, etc. Repair spares are those which you predict you will need. I carry a CV joint, a clutch, a spare water pump and hoses, oil seals, brake master cylinder, etc. And because I run larger than normal tyres I carry a lot of Timken bearings. Landy drivers – don't use the Blue Brand with A Bad Name for anything mechanical. Plastic stuff sure, but nothing else. Use Bearmach dammit!

8. Work slowly and methodically, do not rush. Keep all the parts clean and free of moisture and dirt, clean each part and take pride in your work. After years on the road, doing all the maintenance and repairs roadside or in a campsite, a flat, level concrete surface is a joy for us. You always drop the little bastard nuts and bolts and when working over dirt or grass that can mean wasted time lying on your belly digging around. A little magnetic nuts n bolts dish can be a great metal detector and helps keep things organised

9. Take a slow test drive and be sure that your repair is good before permanently leaving the safety of your repair area. Keep the old part if it is still semi-usable and only discard when you have run the new part for long enough to be confident. We once changed some bad wheel bearings in Brazil, but luckily kept the old bearings in the spares crate. 1000km's down the road the new Blue Brand bearings imploded and had I not kept the old bearings, we would not have been able to limp back to the nearest town

10. When done with maintenance or repairs, clean your tools and pack everything in its correct place. This you can do while sipping on a well deserved beer while your significant other is preparing the meat for the fire. Breakdowns are a great time to spoil yourself, it keeps moral high and you can justify the expense by calculating how much you have saved by not using a mechanic. Beer and meat and fire and grease. This is an adventure, right?

A special thank you to Bill Rayner for taking me under his wing and teaching me how to take care of my Defender.

Travel The Planet Overland

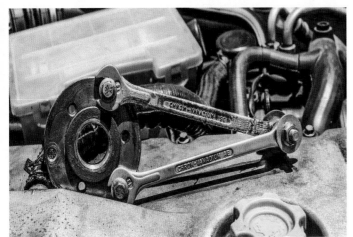

Off-road Driving & Recovery Techniques

As with vehicle maintenance, and most things in life, prevention is better than cure. You will need to practice the different driving techniques required for technically challenging surfaces if you intend to take your home on wheels off the black stuff. The rule is, "as fast as necessary and as slow as possible". This is the mature off-road driving technique. Then there is the, "peddle to the metal" technique favoured by the cowboy crowd, this technique involves tackling all obstacles with maximum power and, if stuck, spinning your wheels and swaying the steering wheel until the exhausted vehicle finds some traction and works its way out. Mechanical sensitivity is very important for an overlander who is driving his home, not a weekend toy. Destroying your clutch, CV and U Joints or overheating your engine in a remote off road situation is, in many cases, a recipe for disaster.

Here are a few tips to avoid getting bogged down and for vehicle recovery. Land Rover drivers need only read this as a reference for helping others (again, I am kidding of course).

Water crossings

- Assess the water obstacle. Can you see the far bank? Are there tyre tracks entering and exiting the water? Is there an upside down weed strewn Toyota downstream? How fast is the water flowing and what material is most likely to be under the water, mud, stone or sand?

- When in doubt, walk it out. Never drive through suspect water without first sending the wife for a swim or getting your own feet wet. If you are lucky enough and have successfully implemented the TIC (Travel Indoctrination Campaign), your significant other will become the designated Spotter and will volunteer to stumble around in the croc infested waters while you sip on a cold one

- Walk the line of both the left and right tyres, you want to be sure that there are no invisible large holes or washouts

- Be prepared to wait out a fast moving river, sometimes there has been rain upstream, perhaps far away, which temporarily swells the river. The water level may drop eventually, make a cup of tea and have some lunch, do not camp too close to the water's edge, have a look around for an indication of a high water mark or flood level. Camping in a dry river bed can be dangerous if there is rain predicted. A flash flood can be deadly and may destroy your vehicle

- If having walked the water you are still in doubt wait for a local to come along. He will arrive in a beat up old sedan full of very large women and drive across without batting an eye. You will feel pretty silly, don't stress about it. If the local pulls up, shakes his head, makes a u turn and disappears back down the road, follow him. Find a place to camp or look for another route, one with a bridge perhaps

- Let the engine cool before doing a deep water crossing, a hot engine will not react well to the sudden cooling effect of the water
Those with motorised transport must be aware of the height of the engines air intake.

- Diesel engines tend to cope better with water ingress than petrol engines. If you have a petrol engine, spray the points, coil, spark plugs and other electrical components in the engine bay with a good dose of WD40, Q20 or similar which will repel the water and prevent a stall half way through. If the vehicle stalls and you did not spray the components with the lubricant, now would be a good time to do it if the water is not too deep and the engine is not submerged. A raised air intake, or snorkel, permanently attached to the vehicle is a sound investment, not only for water crossings but also for raising the air intake away from the dust churned up by your wheels

- If water enters the engine and the vehicle stalls, DO NOT try and start the engine, you may destroy it, try and winch yourself out, bearing in mind that the battery may run dead without the engine running to power it

- Bikers should carry tools and knowledge to unflood the engine if water ingress occurs

- Enter deep water slowly, in low range second if possible, and increase your speed gradually until you create a bow wave with the vehicle. The vehicle will push the water forward and depressions will be created behind the wave which will decrease the resistance to the vehicle and prevent the water from entering the vehicle. Driving through water deeper than the top of your bonnet is unadvisable especially if the water is flowing swiftly

- If you have no choice but to cross the fast flowing, deep water, perhaps an angry father or boyfriend is chasing you, take the time to attach the winch controller and spool out the winch cable and attach it to your roof rack. This way you will not have to go diving for your winch should you get stuck. Usually there are trees where there are rivers but not always. You might have to improvise a sand anchor
- Give the vehicle a good run after a significant water crossing, the heat and movement will expel residual water and moisture from the engine, clutch and chassis. That moisture could cause problems with the electrical components the next morning
- Cyclists, wait for a truck to give you a ride across or risk swimming it with your bike if you are stronger than the current. Holding onto a wet, heavy bike in a strong current is like oil wrestling an anaconda. Good luck.

Sand driving

If you love the beach as much as we do, you might find yourself doing a lot of sand driving; depending on the vehicle you drive. Or you might be one of those strange people who get a thrill from a remote desert. Much of the sand you will encounter is going to be thick and soft. Here are a few tips...

- Momentum is everything. That said the, "as fast as necessary and as slow as possible" rule still applies. Go too slow and you may bog down, go too fast and you may lose control or go shooting off the crest of a dune and nose dive into another
- A general rule is the hotter the climate the softer the sand; the cooler the climate the firmer the sand
- You may need to air down your tyres if the sand is particularly soft and you are driving with skinny biscuit tyres. Remember, deflating your tyres will provide a larger footprint, hence more flotation and grip. A large tyre already has a large foot print, but may still need to be deflated. We have driven on many beaches with our 33 / 12.5 R15 tyres fully inflated
- In deep, soft sand we drive in low range throughout the gears, starting in second gear
- If driving on a bank and the vehicle begins to list heavily to the side, in danger of rolling, steer downhill into the roll, DO NOT attempt to turn up, though this is instinctual. By turning into the roll, and accelerating as necessary, you will disperse the inertia and prevent a dangerous and costly roll over, you may end up in a precarious position, off the track and surrounded by walls of sand but your vehicle will be intact, on all four wheels and your necks and skulls uncracked
- As soon as the vehicle loses momentum and becomes stationary with spinning wheels, take your foot off the accelerator, DO NOT continue to spin the wheels until the vehicle is buried in the sand, up to its chassis. If you have differential lockers, engage them and attempt to reverse. If you are able to regain traction and free the vehicle, continue forwards with more power and perhaps following a different line. If the vehicle remains

stuck, it is time to do some work. Using a spade, remove sand from in front of and behind the wheels and behind the differentials, we want to reduce any drag. We know what the terrain is like behind us and depending on the type of terrain, it may be easier to reverse. Lay sand ladders, palm fronds, fire wood or even the vehicle foot mats behind or in front of the wheels depending on which direction you intend to drive. If your tyres have not been deflated, or only partially, now is the time to let some air out. Passengers are now invited to push and rock the vehicle as you drive out in low range with all lockers engaged. Keep going until you find a more solid piece of ground, then return on foot to recover your equipment

- If you are still not able to recover the vehicle and have a winch, now may be the time to use it. Chances are there will be nothing sturdy enough to winch off. If you have a sand anchor you can use it or you will have to improvise. Unfortunately, you are unlikely to have a winch at the rear of the vehicle so you will have to go forwards. Take your spare wheel and your high lift jack if you have one, carry them about twenty meters from your rig, dig a deep hole, attach the winch cable and toss the spare and jack in the hole then cover with sand. Twist a jacket or rope around the middle of the winch cable, start the engine, open the bonnet to protect you and the windscreen should the cable snap and winch after clearing the sand from the tyres and the differentials. You should also use the sand ladders etc, engage low range, diff lockers and first or second gear and slowly turn the wheels

- If you are accompanied by another vehicle, they could recover you using a tow or snatch strap. The snatch strap uses kinetic energy and is not meant to be used at high speeds, ensure that the straps are connected to designated recovery points on the bumpers or bull bar

- If you remain stuck and there is no one to help, you may have to go looking for help or continue to use a combination of methods to free the vehicle. Remember to stay calm, hydrate, wear a hat and apply sunscreen. Chances are someone will come along to help you. If you do leave the vehicle, follow your tracks back to where you came from. This is the worst case scenario and will probably never happen

- Stop or park the vehicle on down hills as you will be able to pull off with the aid of gravity

- Remember to inflate the tyres when back on solid ground.

Recovering Others

There exist these mystical beings we call, The Gods of the Road. They are always watching and they really, truly believe in enforcing Karma, so chances are they are Buddhist or closely related to Buddha. You want to appease these chaps in order to ensure that you get some of the good stuff in return. Yes, helping others is a completely selfish act. If you come across a stranded or stuck fellow motorist in a remote area, it is your duty to assist them if they are unlikely to receive any other assistance. Be careful though, some criminals have been known to fake a road side emergency and then rob good Samaritans who stop to help. It is difficult to believe that such upright faeces exist but, unfortunately, they do. Helping fellow overlanders is mandatory.

But, there may be downsides to recovering a stuck vehicle. Like the great Hawaiian life guard Brian L Keaulana said, "you can rush into a situation where a person is drowning, and you rush in, now there's two persons drowning". Fans of Riding Giants just grinned.

- It is important to assess the situation before getting involved
- You may find as you travel that you will be using your winch to recover other people more than to recover yourself
- Usually the person you are helping is a local who may have other resources available or friends he can call
- If you are going to recover another vehicle be sure that you take control of the situation and supervise the attachment of the cables and D shackles
- Do not endanger your vehicle by entering rough terrain to reach the stricken vehicle. If you have a winch with an extension, you can attempt to recover the other vehicle from the safety of solid ground
- Be careful not to do damage to your vehicle
- Be sure that everyone stands a safe distance away from the vehicles recovering and being recovered
- Do not feel obligated to rescue a vehicle if you feel that the situation is too dangerous
- The driver of the vehicle being recovered will be responsible for the purchase of beers or a bottle of whiskey once the work is done.

Travelling with Children

Time to get that bottle of wine out

I met a wonderful couple at a recent Overland Expo held in Flagstaff, Arizona. This is the second time we have met and I am glad we did. They are just so wonderfully enthusiastic, kind and engaging, that the cynical bugger living in my skin was convinced after the first meeting that they were "taking the piss", to quote the English. They were not. They are so similar in positive vibe, athletically fresh, wide eyed wonderment, that I at first assumed that they were siblings, not lovers. The planets must have collided gently and with a warm embrace when they first met, two souls so wonderful and rare that it could not be anything less than a miracle that the two met. They feed off each others positivity, they encourage each other and are strong, brave, beautiful and everything we all want to be. I want to meet their parents.

We used to be ordinary people, to be honest, we still are. Back in the pre-overlanding, suburban bliss life we loathed but worked so hard to achieve, we went through the daily cycles spun by the vast majority of the world's people. We woke up reluctantly, forced the children to wake and fought to dress them in the colours of their school, pouring cereal down their throats and dropping them off at the gates of an institution where people indoctrinated in the philosophy of the collective waited impatiently to squeeze every last drop of the individual out of those sweet, innocent souls. If those souls resisted the constant daily onslaught, we, the parents, would then be pressured by the collective, resistance is futile, conform or you will be banished. By now you will realise that we certainly did not live in Scandinavia.

We chose exile and were liberated. We chose to be responsible for our children's education and we chose to take full responsibility for the outcome of our actions. Besides, I once asked a particularly obnoxious headmaster (think about that title for a moment) to take responsibility for the failings of his school and he responded by telling me that I, as the parent, am the child's primary educator and therefore I must assume full responsibility for my child's failures and the school, presumably, will take the credit for his success. Well, that's that then, no more school fees and constant notes demanding involvement, contribution, charity and assimilation.

They say that the accountant's son becomes a hippie and the hippie's son becomes an accountant. Often a father will encourage his child to follow in his footsteps because he has walked the path for many years and can guide his child through a career. It was good enough for me son, it will bloody well be good enough for you. Many sons rebel, rejecting the paternal path, criticising the father for settling, for being a hypocrite, emboldened by the certainty of youth, desperate to be their own man, unaware what the father has had to sacrifice in order to be a good father, in order to do what he should, in order to provide.

We have decided to work to our children's strengths instead of trying to choose a path for them. Our son is left handed, mathematically minded and intrigued by architecture, technology, archaeology and food. Our daughter learnt how to read and write in a matter of weeks and has a way with words and animals, her touch reduces any beast to adoring servitude. We have provided them with a results driven curriculum of Maths and English (which will enable them to write exams and qualify to attend universities in either Norway or Slovenia where higher education is free, even for foreigners), all other skills are learnt through their adventurous lifestyle and through the amazing people they meet while on the road. They have become friends with scientists and millionaires, aviators and artists, potters and mechanics, bankers and soldiers and the intentionally homeless. They will not be shown the "door" when they come of age, instead they will be encouraged to stay with the tribe, to contribute and to leave when they are ready and return at will.

And if one day someone meets them and cynically refuses to believe that anyone so wonderful truly exists, then the wife and I will have done our work well, we would have parented with love and wisdom and we would have given our children the key to true success.

If you have children and plan to road raise them this chapter is for you. There are a few ways to educate your children while travelling and there are a million opinions regarding the responsible upbringing and education of overlander kids. Some parents choose to travel before their children are of school going age and then return to the real world in time for their kids to enrol. A minority of parents will send the kids to boarding schools (sometimes a very tempting option) while they continue to travel while others will "home" school the children to a set curriculum, whether paper based or computer based or both. Some will opt for a mix home schooling and real world "experiential" schooling and another minority will "unschool" their kids, an education based almost purely on experiences and self-motivated learning. The responsibility is significant, you are making choices now for your children which will determine their entire futures, a mistake in the fundamental phases of education could lead to years of struggle.

We chose to educate our children with a mix of home schooling and real world "experiential" schooling. We first took them out of school in 2010 for six months and returned them to school until 2012 when we removed them permanently.

I will admit that 52% of the allure of overlanding long-term, is that I would get to spend every day with my children and have the opportunity to watch them grow and participate in their lives as their primary educator, along with Luisa. I was not happy with the schools which they had attended back in South Africa and they had been to both expensive private schools and public schools. In my experience the public schools, actually provided a superior service to the results driven, pill prescribing private schools. It broke my heart to drop my kids off at school every day. Bullying is a massive problem which is never correctly addressed by schools. There simply are not enough attentive adults employed in most schools to monitor the behaviour of problem children; children who have horrible, perhaps violent, home lives which they mimic in their interaction with other children.

Your life philosophy, and wealth, will go a long way in determining how your children will be raised and educated but whatever you choose, you have to believe in the process and the path and you have to be committed to your children's intellectual growth. But wealth is not the single most important factor. You can provide your children with the latest high tech tools to learn but if you are unable to motivate them your money and time is wasted. What you need is patience, a huge, bottomless pit of the stuff. Having been on the road for a number of years, homeschooling throughout the entire period, we have learnt that life on the road is the best education a child can receive. No one is going to give them a certificate for learning what they have but they will carry that knowledge with them for life.

Let me give you a few examples of what our kids have learnt as junior overlanders...

- They can communicate in four languages
- They have met and become friends with many highly qualified and interesting people from all walks of life, adventurers, pilots, doctors, engineers, cancer researchers, entrepreneurs, scientists, etc.
- They have learnt geography with all their senses
- They know how to repair their own gear
- They have learnt to navigate by map and using technology
- They have learnt about cultures and the folly of racism
- They have learnt to live off the grid
- They have learnt the value of money
- They have learnt to self-motivate
- They have learnt how to work, mentally and physically.

All of that is the tip of the iceberg. Almost everyone we meet says the same thing, "what an education". It truly is the best thing we have ever done for ourselves and our children, we are learning as much as they are! Perhaps the One lesson we need our children to learn is that the impossible is not impossible. You can do almost anything if you set out with the correct expectations and believe that you CAN.

There are a few resources available with regards to a structured home schooling curriculum for your children. It must be noted that if you're looking at travelling away from major routes, you may not have access to the internet and this is when a good paper or computer based curriculum will come in handy. As mentioned previously, the South African curriculum leaves a lot to be desired with little or no imagination left to the learner. Any modular based curriculum will suffice, as this will enable the child to learn at his own pace. If you wish to educate your children in all the subjects, i.e. Biology, Science, Economics etc. it would be suggestible to contact a Private Home Schooling provider in your country of residence, to purchase their curriculum. The following are resources available internationally. We cannot vouch for any of the undermentioned institutions but are aware that they exist as a resource.

Hence, it's a short list based almost purely on reputation:

KhanAcademy.org – personally my favourite of all the resources available
Sonlight.com – Christian based
Amblesideonline.org
EdX
Code.org
Dadsworksheets.com – printable worksheets
Illuminations.nctm.org
Sumdog.com

Travelling over a long period with children has, with all things in life, its pros and cons. Younger children may struggle to be helpful around the camp simply because their arms and legs are too short and they do not have the strength or coordination to perform many tasks even though they really want to help. Older children, while more capable, are generally less motivated to be helpful and may need constant motivation. For the overlander family, privacy is a rare and elusive bird. You will be spending almost every moment of every day together, sharing every meal and experience and space which, in the beginning of the journey, can be very stressful. However, you will soon fall into a routine and begin to bond in a way that you never have before. Without the distractions of normal life, the family unit can grow stronger and closer until you all become seamless, merely parts of a greater whole. If anything, this is the natural state of the family as for many thousands of years the family has worked closely together for survival and mutual benefit, each member of the family had clear roles and responsibilities.

That does not mean that conflict will completely disappear. Sibling rivalry can be an endless source of conflict and frustration which is compounded by the fact that the children will very often have no interaction with other children for long, boring periods of time. A love hate relationship can develop which will lead to bickering all bloody day long then falling asleep in each other's arms. Chores, such as dish washing and laundry are catalysts for tears and sulking, particularly when the other kid only had to wash four plates and this kid has to wash up after a large complicated meal. You are doing your children a favour by having them do daily chores. They will grow up to be better people for the experience and will be more respectful and capable. Remember this. Of all the regrets I will have in my old age I do not think I will ever regret taking my children out of school and raising them on the road, living in a Land Rover. If anything I will look back as the life drains out of my grey, wrinkled body and applaud myself for having the balls to follow my dreams and spend the best years of my children's life, and therefore the best years of my life, by their sides, always available, always there. They might regret me not being more responsible with my money during my most productive years as they count the cost of caring for aging parents but, we are African, we invest in our children now so that they can care for us later. "I don't mean to be a burden but who took your ungrateful butt around the planet? Now, hand me that catheter".

The joy and laughter generated by a happy family is enviable. We joke and sing and laugh and tease each other endlessly. Our tent is a happy, cosy nest, side by side we dream and cuddle through the cold nights or enjoy the breeze on the hot, humid nights. Yes, privacy is in short supply but there are a few things you can do to ensure that everyone has enough personal time...

- Have a separate small ground tent which mom and dad can use or the kids can sleep in if camped in a safe, secure camp
- Mom and Dad should try and have a date night when reliable baby sitters present themselves
- The Retired Couple make great baby sitters
- Rent a two or three-bedroom apartment or cottage once every few months
- Seek campsites run by friendly families and introduce the kids, they will keep each other busy for many hours
- Take turns baby sitting with other overlanding parents
- Be honest with your kids, tell them that Mom and Dad need some alone time if the marriage is to last, tell them to go play in the trees until they are called.

There are several ways to entertain your children while on the road. We usually play these on the road:

Mini Scrabble
The Land Rover game – different scores for spotting Land Rovers
The Silent game – The first one to speak loses, a classic
Uno
Word Association.

There are several other programmes and/or games available on the internet, these are the very few our children utilise:

Horrible Histories
BBC – has many documentaries available
Ebooks – Kobo
Audiobooks – Librivox
Minecraft.

Toys

Unless you have small children, aged 0 to 18 months, you need not pack every soft toy, Lego piece or toy car they own. There are many stores that cater to young children and a lot of toys take ample space. They are also very difficult to keep in one place, at a time. Grab a bag, preferably durable but with mesh, so that you can shake out all the dirt and critters that gather when they have been playing with it in the sand, the forest or on the beach. When in a mesh bag, you can also hose down the entire toy collection in one go. When our children were still young, we made them a deal. Once the toy started showing wear and tear, we would buy them a new one or replace it with another toy, if they gave up one or more in trade. The older toys would be handed over to a local child, who in all likelihood could not afford to have that specific Barbie or A Team doll or Hot Wheels car and would take care of it until the next less fortunate kid came along. Lego pieces are fantastic to have. They are very compact, cater to both boys and girls and you can set up a challenge for your kids to build something spectacular for a treat.

Stay away from any noisy toys with blinking lights. As a mother, I was inclined to accept all toys from the grandparents but that ended once we hit the road. They may be cute to your mother who decided her grandchild needed some "real" entertainment but I can assure you, it will be turfed and there will be tears.

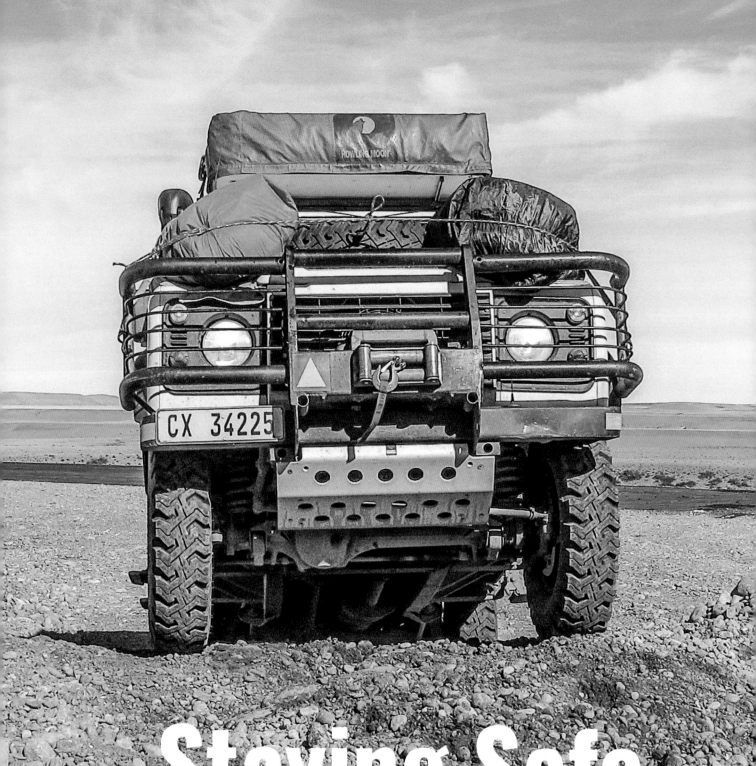

Staying Safe

The greatest obstacle to most people achieving their dreams is not lack of wealth or health or a set of nice strong teeth. It is fear. Fear of the unknown, fear of leaving the comfort zone, fear of the future. The only way to overcome that fear is to try something new and to do it with the correct mental attitude. A positive attitude makes everything better and easier. When we travel we do not look down at people from behind tinted windows. We do not treat poor, hard working people with disrespect or contempt. We try to be patient when faced with a trying situation and we do not let ourselves be provoked. Except for that one time in Mexico but, man, that guy really got on my nerves (and he did not have ten buddies waiting in the wings for a dust up).

When travelling overland you can expect corrupt police and military checkpoints, locals who are sick of rich stuck up tourists and drunk people. Lots and lots of drunk people. When faced with an aggressive or negative person you need to stay calm and approach the situation with resolution in mind. No, you don't pay bribes, ever and do not assume that every policeman or soldier is corrupt. Since we are in a list making mood, lets make a list.

1. Overreacting to a bad situation only makes it worse. You are outnumbered in a foreign land or town. As long as you behave respectfully and confidently without being arrogant, you should be able to walk or drive away from almost any situation
2. Drive carefully and defensively with the anticipation that every other road user is half drunk, totally stoned or fast asleep. Watch out for pedestrians, cyclists, untethered livestock and small children carrying buckets of water. Buses and trucks are the kings of the road due to their sheer size and drive accordingly. When driving through towns and cities obey all the road signals without fault and do not drive like the locals. Always come to a full stop at stop streets and yield when necessary. You do not want to give the police an excuse to stop you
3. When stopped at a police checkpoint or pulled over by a policeman and it is obvious that they are angling for a bribe go through the following procedure:
   - Smile and stay calm
   - Hand over your documentation when asked, paperwork is replaceable
   - Pretend that you do not speak the local language, unless you don't then you're good
   - If the policeman is fat you are in for a bit of bother. The fatter the policeman the more bother. He is hungry and you are a rich tourist. He is planning to have something special for dinner and he expects you to pay for it
   - He will hold onto your drivers license or passport and inform you of an infraction. You pretend that you do not understand
   - He will tell you that the fine is huge, you will not understand If he insists that you pay a fine say ok and show him with hand signals that he must write you a fine – this may not apply to European license holders travelling across Europe
   - If he writes a ticket take it, say thank you, retrieve your documentation, drive away and use the ticket to start the campfire that night. There is no traffic department in any country that we have toured which is linked to customs and immigration. They will not know that you have outstanding fines when you leave or re-enter the country
   - If he does not issue a ticket but insists that you pay then and there, pretend not to understand. Remember, you have all the time in the world, even if you do not
   - Do not get angry. Your humility ensures your safety. Shouting at a policeman elevates

a traffic infringement into misconduct

- At this stage you are heading for check mate. Get out of the vehicle and stand in front of the vehicle, cross your arms, look unhappy. Other motorists will see that you are being harassed and the policeman will probably lose his nerve. He will return your documents and tell you to bugger off. Thank him and drive away

4. Establish your priorities. What is more important to you, your possessions or your life? In the event of an armed robbery you need to assess the threat, if he is a little man with a dull knife, on his own, proceed to break his nose and crack his skull if you are good at violence. Then drive away. If he is a little man with a big gun, hand over whatever he wants as soon as the kids or wife or friend or pet is out of the vehicle, if he wants the vehicle. Take charge of the situation by being calm

5. Always keep a large denomination note in a pocket away from your wallet for emergency situations

6. Stay in camp at night. Unless you are in a place where you feel safe or are with people you trust, avoid driving at night and going to nightclubs. The bad guys come out at night because they enjoy the cover of darkness. Rather hang out around the campfire, have a beer and tan some meat

7. Don't do drugs. Too many travellers die because they want to party. You will meet a friendly guy who will help you get some weed. Enjoy said weed around the campfire, if that is your thing

8. Do not overload your vehicle. OK, we all know you will overload it, just do not overload it too much.

We don't carry a firearm and we don't suggest you do either. We do however have a hunting knife, a few handy pepper sprays and two machetes. Keep them in a handy spot and if you feel unsafe in a camp, take it up the RTT or in your sleeping area. Better prepared than not

Travel The Planet Overland

$how
me the
money

Liberation Initiatives

By now you have had a good look at your finances, have motivated your significant other, decided on a mode of transportation, have learnt how to keep the wheels rolling, assessed your gear requirements and addressed your fears with a plan for safety. Now we need to move on to the process of leaving your calm, safe life behind and hitting the road.

Organise your life

If you are wealthy, inform your inner circle of your plans to depart. They will provide you with free gear and an invitation to stay in their holiday homes around the planet, they will offer you all insurance and technology you will need as a going away present. Because you are rich, you will hardly need to pay for anything, this is how I assume wealth works.

The poorer you are the more planning and organisation you will need to do. Unless you are single and have just enough funds for a return flight and a bicycle, then you will have to be a moocher Cyclist. Generally, the older you are, the more likely you are to have a complicated web of income and debt and contracts and obligations, not to mention a lot of stuff. The following Liberation Initiatives, or LI's, will certainly help with the preparation for extraction...

- Manage your debt. This should be done way in advance and is a habit which will serve you well in real life, whether you decide to become a long-term traveller or not. It is best to have a few credit cards with large credit limits and low balances. Pay cash for whatever you can and keep debt to an absolute minimum. These credit cards will provide a safety buffer if the wheels come off, literally and figuratively

- Sell what you do not need or use and be very careful with the purchase of new gear. It is very easy to waste thousands on gimmicky gear which you will never need and will hardly ever use. Invest in high quality products which are durable and used daily

- Simplify your life. Overlanders are usually minimalists by nature and being a minimalist will not only save you a lot of money but will also make your life happier and less cluttered. It is true that your possessions own you. Cancel all unnecessary subscriptions and contracts, sell the TV and the satellite dish, watch movies on your laptop. Empty your home of clutter and crap. A garage sale or online auction will turn all that unwanted clutter into travel money

- Those possessions which you are simply unwilling to part with will need to find a temporary home when you leave. If you have a lot of stuff, buy a used shipping container and find a relative with a large piece of land. Pack everything in there, warm and dry, to await your eventual return. You will be able to sell the container for almost what you paid for it when you eventually return, though you will more than likely turn the container into a little house and will live a simple life, watering a vegetable garden after a kale smoothie and a yoga session

- Accumulate as much money as possible in the months or years before you leave. Harass your debtors, put in extra shifts, take on a second job, buy and sell diamonds on the black market, invent an app or two, sell your body but not your soul. Whatever it takes

- Accumulate US Dollars, Great British Pounds and Euros, particularly if you are from a country where these currencies are foreign. The powers that be use those currencies to conduct the global economy and you want to back a winning horse.

If you begin early enough with the above LI's you will be in great financial condition when the day of departure arrives.

Paperwork

Ensure that all your relevant paperwork, be it passports, carnets, medical insurance etc. have been scanned and stored on an Internet server for instance Dropbox, Google Drive or OneDrive. You will need to ensure that all your paperwork is in order before you leave and that all your credit cards have been renewed, your life policies are up to date and any insurance is paid up. Make sure that you have appointed a family member as a signatory on your accounts, as you may need them to assist in procuring new credit cards and this way, they can collect them and forward them to you without any hassle.

Try to ensure that your motor vehicle documentation is in order and that you have arranged for your family member to either settle any renewals personally or that you have set up a payment method that you can do remotely. Try not to deregister your vehicle, you will require the documentation to remain valid for a carnet and shipping purposes.

- Before you depart you will need to invest in some medical insurance if travelling abroad especially where public health care is available but not an option
- In South Africa you are able to get free medical treatment at any number of state run hospitals or clinics, unfortunately the standard is extremely low and anyone who can afford it will turn to the expensive but excellent private medical institutions
- Ensure that you read all the terms and conditions of your health cover. Some companies will not renew your medical insurance for a period longer than a year without returning home. Some will rather fly you home, to get treated by your own medical system than settle a huge medical bill (particularly in the USA)
- Pre-existing conditions are a nightmare and many claims are denied because of this
- There are some reputable companies for instance, World Nomads, AIG, do some research, ask fellow overlanders. We found most Latin Americans countries have great medical and dental care, at very low costs. Some African states have good public care but in all honesty, we ensured we carried our own syringes when travelling in Africa and most medical facilities are not very sanitary
- If you need to get medical care in a developing nation, find out where foreign diplomats go for assistance, diplomats will only use the best medical care facilities.

The Back Up Guy

Just because you are hitting the road and leaving normal life behind does not necessarily mean that normal life is done with you. You will still need to file tax returns, receive and dispose of mail, make financial transactions and renew bureaucratic necessities such as vehicle documentation, driver licenses and passports. If you have the resources to fly home once every six months you may be able to take care of these matters with little assistance but chances are you are going to need someone "on the inside" to keep you from falling foul of the financial and governments structures to which you are obligated.

Your Back Up Guy needs to be intelligent, motivated, trust worthy, competent and preferably, blood. Remember, when you announce that you are heading off to travel the planet your friends and family will be amazed and in awe. Then they will have some quiet time and a think. They will wonder how you came to be so rich, they will wonder why you have not shared that wealth with them, they will ponder why you have not invited them along for the ride and they will eventually settle on a belief that you have come by your resources and resolve by pure luck, that you are going on a silly long-term holiday while they have to continue fighting the good fight. They will wish you well and maybe like a few of your overlanding snaps on Facebook.

Your Back Up Guy needs to be someone who truly loves you, who has been with you through thick and thin and who respects what you are going to be doing for the unforeseeable future. You will need to be able to trust this person with your bank account, PIN and password. Think about that for a moment. With internet banking you are able to manage your finances from anywhere in the world but there are limitations to what can be done remotely for an extended period of time and with all the banking fraud going on the banks are particularly wary of suspect activities in far flung corners of the globe.

Your trusty Back Up Guy's duties may include:

- Sending and receiving post on your behalf
- Purchasing products, ie car parts, electronic equipment, beloved snacks, packaging them and forwarding the parcel to whichever country you may be holed up in
- Applying for and receiving new credit and debit cards in advance of the expiry on the current cards, and shipping those securely to you
- Making enquiries and submissions on your behalf at the relevant tax authorities
- Management and storage of your few remaining worldly possessions
- Renewal of vehicle documentation
- Storage of back up documentation such as certified copies of birth and marriage certificates, passport and national identification card
- Creating a frantic "help find them" Facebook page when you have been off the grid for week without telling anyone that you will be off the grid or in the case of your actual, legitimate disappearance.

The relationship with the Back Up Guy must be carefully maintained. Remember, they have their own crap to deal with and may not fully comprehend the urgency of certain requests,

particularly if they have never been overlanding or even to another country. Perhaps the solution is to invest in the Back Up Guy relationship long before you actually leave on your journey. Take them along for a road trip or two to experience how you will be living once on the road permanently. If they understand how vulnerable you can sometimes be they will be more inclined to be more urgently helpful when the proverbial hits the fan and you are very far away and in need. When on the road have them fly in and join you for a week of "soft" overlanding, maybe rent a cabin in the hills and treat the Back Up Guy to a slice of your new life. Once they are part of your journey, your needs will become their needs and you will both benefit from the relationship.

Or you could hire an attorney.

Apart from your regular income stream there are a few options available to help cover costs both back home and while you are on the road. This is a hot topic, many blogs and articles have been written about how to earn and travel. Essentially you will need to work out a daily, monthly and annual budget in relation to your travel goals. Then you will need to live by that budget and supplement it where possible when necessary. We can get by on USD60 per day as a family of four, including a very large and hungry teenager and a very large and thirsty patriarch. This amount includes camping, fuel and food, repair, maintenance and sundry costs. When in Europe and the USA, this amount increases by 30%.

The following tips will help you to save money while travelling...

- Volunteer as you travel. Volunteering is unpaid casual work, usually on a farm or ranch similar to Israeli Kibbutz volunteers. You do a few hours work each day and receive food and board as compensation. You will get to learn new skills and cultures and make some new friends. Be sure to research volunteer opportunities, try not to become someone's servant in Saudi Arabia

- House sitting is a good option for clean, tidy, respectful and reliable people. There are house sitting gigs available in many countries around the globe. This is a great opportunity to live like the locals do and rent free for a few weeks or even a few months. It is important to get good references for any house sitting assignments you do. A great rule of thumb is to leave the property in a better condition than when you found it. There are websites whose soul function is to introduce sitters to owners and the investment to join is only a few dollars. You could see the world by working remotely while house sitting

- Become a vegetarian. Eat meat on special occasions and buy your fruit and vegetables from the local markets. You will be thin and healthy in no time and will save a lot of money. We regard Monday to Monday as a special occasion, we do not save a lot of money

- If you insist on being a carnivore eat the cuts the locals eat. The world loves a good roasted chicken. Western style steaks are usually very expensive unless you are in Southern Africa

- Cook your own food. Eating out can be hugely expensive particularly in industrialised countries

Reduce your alcohol consumption. For the first few months on the road this may be easier said than done. Firstly, you will want to celebrate your new found freedom then you will make some new friends who will want to help you celebrate. Then you will realise that every day is Saturday. It is a slippery slope

Free camp as much as possible. We have met people who only ever stay in campsites and we have met others who never pay to camp. If you can sleep in your rig, it is relatively easy to free camp in most countries. We are huge fans of camping at rural gas stations. There is usually a 24 hour guard and bathrooms while some of the larger gas stations which cater to long distance truckers might even have hot showers and restaurants. You could also free camp in the wild, far from any settlements but this takes a bit more courage, it depends on the potential hostility of the country you are in. Having an overland rig which is designed for you to sleep inside and access the drivers seat without leaving the vehicle is perfect for wild and free camping. At any sign of trouble you can hop over, start up and drive away. The investment in this type of set up will be repaid within the first year of overlanding as you will save money every day

Mooch. Be aware though. Mooching can lead to a bad reputation and word spreads faster than you could ever drive or ride. A good practice is to cook for your host if you are invited into someone's home and are likely to be there for a while. Wash dishes and clean up, maybe cut the lawn or wash the windows. Give more than you get and you will never run out of welcoming friends

Repair and reuse. Buy a good pair of shoes and wear them for five years. Repair them until you no longer can. Sew patches in your pants, darn your socks. Live like your grandparents did and take pride in your possessions. You will be surprised how long a good pair of jeans can last. Black shirt looking a little grey, Dye instead Buy. After a while you will begin to look like a true traveller, a patina that can only be earned, never faked. Learn to repair your electronics and other possessions. The overlanding evenings can get boring, especially if you are cutting back on alcohol, use this free time to fix stuff

Grow your hair long or keep it short. Buy a set of Wahl clippers and use it to keep your hair short and to shave the hair on your face. You will not have that Gillette look but you will not be living a life surrounded by mirrors. You might catch a glimpse of yourself in the rigs window and think, "hmm, this travelling lifestyle suits me".

Making money while travelling can be a bit more challenging. Most countries require work permits for foreigners unless if, for example, you are an European Union (EU) passport holder travelling in the EU and are able to work without specific paperwork. The top on the road money makers would be...

Working remotely online. Many IT professionals are able to work remotely but are dependent on decent internet connectivity. If you are a geek in a jeep you can live cheaply, travel and work and return home with a bank account full of cash

Teaching English as a Foreign Language or TEFL as it is commonly known. The idea here would be that you travel for six months then work for six months then travel for six ad nauseam. If English is your first language and you have a high school diploma you can do an online course and qualify within a month as an English teacher. With English being the global business language there is no shortage of opportunities to travel and teach. South East Asia and South America are great TEFL destinations

Bar and restaurant work. If you have experience waiting tables, serving drinks or making food, you can do quite well in certain upmarket areas. We have a Belgian friend who made excellent food and he had struck an agreement with a surf camp in Peru to run their little restaurant. Word got around that he was the best chef in town and soon he was raking in the cash

Use any transferable desirable skills you may have and teach others, we are thinking about normal, legal things like teaching people to surf or kayak or to program computers or create websites. We are not thinking of robbing banks or cat burglary or paramilitary subterfuge or racketeering. Obviously

Anyone looking to either sell articles and photographs and write books will need to invest in a social media presence. These days an individuals success or popularity is determined by the amount of followers they have on Facebook, Instagram and Twitter. You can budget an allowance for the promotion of your content in order to gain more followers. Personally we have never paid to "boost" our posts or numbers, choosing rather to enjoy organic growth through direct interaction. We find that though we have rather low numbers compared to our peers we have far better interactions and engagements from our followers, even better than those with ten times the followers. We believe in integrity and would never do a "You won't believe what happened next" click bait post. I would rather eat my own hair

There are many ways for photographers to sell their photographs, particularly on the web, or through their own website either as stock photos or even prints sold directly to your followers

By running a blog linked to social media and with the correct SEO settings you will be able to reach an audience which is particularly interested and invested in your type of journey. Focus on what makes you unique, be it your awesome vehicle, your family or companions or, if you really have to, your girlfriends great ass

Writers need a great story and the interest earned through great experiences. There are many online and print publications dedicated to adventure travel and all are competing for content. Most will pay a decent fee for your articles and photos and with time, experience and popularity those fees may increase. You need to be professional in the provision of your content, making it simple for editors to adapt your work for publication. Once you have been published it will be easier to find other platforms for your work. Beware editors who swop "exposure" for content. You cannot eat exposure, but there are times where the publication has significant influence and reach for you to consider the trade off of effort

for social media advances

Self publishing books can lead to a steady income though it is a very difficult and time consuming process. A good book can take months of hard work and dedication to successfully complete and there is no guarantee that the sales will be as meteoric as you expect without significant marketing efforts both before and after publishing. The first rule is this, do not write a crap book. The guru's say that you will not make any money from your first self published book, only after the second or third will you start to see any real income. Our experience with our first book, We Will Be Free, both confirms and contradicts this trend. At first the sales were slow and steady but a year after the book was first published we found that, through a combination of constant "slow boil" marketing and word of mouth the sales have continued to grow and are almost doubling each month. Amazon and their print partner, Createspace take a huge chunk out of the profits and offer absolutely no valuable marketing tools, but if you are prepared to facilitate the orders personally through Createspace, you are able to earn a larger percentage. Printing your books through a printer and selling them out of hand will earn you significantly more income however you will need to carry that stock and find a way to both sell directly out of hand and deliver those books internationally, not easy when you live in a vehicle with limited space and load carrying capabilities. We could write an entire book solely about the self publishing process. Perhaps we should.

With this advice, further strengthening your resolve to hit the road and considering all the other wonderful advice we have given you, it is now time to hand in your notice at work or finalise the sale of your business. Do not burn any bridges by doing something silly like writing "I QUIT" on your buttocks and mooning your boss. Tempting. Ah, what the hell. Go ahead and moon the bugger.

If you are driving from your home to your destination you will have a window of unsettlement and bewilderment as you take the leap from house or apartment dweller.

If you are shipping your vehicle to another continent you will now enter the grey zone.

Shipping

MGW.
TARE
NET
CU.CAP.

There are two types of intercontinental shipping services. RORO, "Roll On Roll Off" and container shipping. Unless you are fabulously wealthy, in which case you can charter a Russian Antonov airplane. Before deciding which option is best for you, consider the following steps:

1. Join a Facebook page or overlander forum relevant to the continent you will be travelling and plead to the God's of last year's trek for advice
2. Ignore 75% of the comments while judiciously searching for the comments of those who have, a) actually travelled the route you are planning and b) are not complete douche bags
3. Search the overlander forums while judiciously searching for the posts of those who have actually travelled the route you are planning and are not complete douche bags
4. Do not be a douche bag
5. You will eventually have a list of recommended shipping agents for the home and away ports and will begin the process of emailing and phoning each for quotations

   Be sure to ask for a breakdown of all costs, including but not limited to...
   - Customs fees
   - Export documentation and filing fees
   - Container costs relevant to the length and height of your vehicle.
   - There are five main types of shipping containers capable of transporting a vehicle, a 20 foot, 40 foot, 40-foot-high cube, 45-foot-high cube and flat rack. A flat rack is best for very large vehicles such as trucks and Unimogs while the high cube containers are best for vehicles no taller than 2.5 meters
   - Receiving, loading, block and brace and unloading fees
   - Drayage and port fees
   - Chassis fee
   - Freight costs
   - Bill of Lading and courier fees
   - Customs clearance
   - Import taxes and duties
   - Insurance
   - Customs inspection charge
   - Terminal Handling Charges
   - Bunker Adjustment Fact

6. Find a shipping partner, usually an overlander heading in the same direction. Splitting the cost of the container in two will save a lot of beer and fuel money
7. RORO ships run in an anti-clockwise direction in the Atlantic. Therefore, shipping from Africa to South America is best done with a container unless you are willing to wait a few months for your beloved vehicle to complete the treacherous circumnavigation
8. Container shipping is safer than RORO shipping as your vehicle is locked inside a sealed container which is usually stacked below hundreds of containers containing thousands of tons of maize, floor tiles, electronics and children toys. With RORO shipping your vehicle is secured to the deck of a ship accessible to Vladimir and Shi-Woo. There have been many reports of overlander vehicles being broken into and picked clean. There have also been many reports of vehicles arriving safely without molestation

9. If shipping to Australia have the vehicle washed and polished, steam cleaned twice inside and out, scrub the chassis and remove ALL dirt, seeds and insects. Inspect every crevice of the vehicle, including behind door panels and floor mats, for residual dirt. Wash and steam clean twice again. Discard any and all foodstuffs and biodegradable matter. Budget to pay the Australian port AUS $700 for cleaning once your rig inevitably fails the inspection
10. RORO tends to be slightly cheaper than container shipping
11. Ensure that you have all your paperwork in order. This will include...
   - A Carnet de Passages en Douane "CPD", which allows a vehicle to be temporarily imported to the country
   - Title deed for the vehicle proving that you are the legal owner of the vehicle
   - Relevant registration papers for your vehicle confirming the VIN (Vehicle Identification Number), Engine Number and number plate
   - Confirmation of insurance

NB. Before you purchase or attempt to ship your vehicle, be sure that the VIN and Engine Number on the registration documentation matches the VIN and Engine Numbers stamped onto the vehicle chassis and engine block respectively. Should those numbers not correspond; your vehicle may have been stolen or rebuilt without following the correct registration procedures. Such a vehicle may, at worst, be confiscated and impounded. The VIN number should be stamped on the chassis behind the wheel in the right front wheel well.

The vehicle is loaded and sailing across the ocean, you have liberated yourself of your worldly possessions and you have booked a ticket to far away shores. Congratulations, you are living the dream!

ON THE ROAD

We will assume, for the sake of assumption, that you have shipped your vehicle across the ocean and have flown for sixteen hours to reunite with your rig and begin that journey you have been dreaming of for so long. You have made it through the airport immigration procedures and are surrounded by foreign sights, sounds and languages, languages which you were supposed to have learnt, but you were so busy extracting yourself from life that you have no more linguistic verbosity than before. You are in the deep end my friend, time to start swimming. Your first task is to learn how the locals live, the real locals, not the people in fancy cars and grand apartments. You want to learn from the people who make their own food, ride bicycles and smile a lot. Local knowledge really is the key to successful budget travel and you can start learning the second you step out of the airport. Most likely you will have a week or two to wait for your ship to come in, literally, and it is during this period of hostel dwelling where you can acclimatise and roam a new city, soaking up all the information like Matt Damon's Jason Bourne. You could also rent an apartment for those few weeks but we would not recommend doing that as you may insulate yourself from the city life and other travellers. Here are a few easy methods for integrating temporarily into a society...

Make friends with a local, maybe someone who wants to learn English. Girls in mini-skirts may be exceptionally friendly but you may find their company expensive. You want to meet someone at the hostel or during a walking tour. Beware of conmen and opportunists and always arrange to hang out with your new friend far from your possessions and valuables

Pay a bit more to stay in a comfortable, upmarket hostel.

1. Many hostels offer free walking tours. Take the tour, if you are lucky the guide will be fun and interesting and will have little nuggets of knowledge the guide books don't possess. Often the guide is an English student making a bit of extra cash, he or she may be interested in having one on one conversations with a native English speaker or may have a friend who needs some help with their vocabulary. An introduction is the best start to a friendship in many cases. At the very least the guide can be a source of local knowledge regarding the best, non-touristy things to do in the city

2. Familiarise yourself with the local currency and prices, by taking a walk through a chain supermarket. You will find that some products are cheaper than back home and some products are more expensive. Look into other people's shopping carts to see what they are buying. Rich people will buy different food to working class people. If there is an attended snack bar ask, "what is that?", "can I try?", "what is that?"," can I try?". You will get a free lunch and you will get to know the names and tastes of snack which you will eat in the future. Even after a year on the road you can walk into a supermarket, point at the snacks, "what is that?", "can I try?". Pretend to like all the snacks and buy a small bag of your favourite. With enough practice this deception can feed a family of four, daily. Do not try this is at a local mom 'n pop store, taking advantage of a giant chain supermarket is fine but not so from common hardworking folk

3. Walk constantly. Take a bus to a beautiful or interesting neighbourhood and simply walk wherever the road leads you, being sure to make mental notes of your route so that you can backtrack, stay away from dark alleys and streets with piles of trash

4. Do not wear a backpack. The locals can get by without one, all you are doing is identifying yourself as a newbie tourist. Carry a small camera, a small amount of cash in local

currency, enough for water and lunch, some form of identification and $100 US hidden in a secret pocket or in the secret pouch in your Leatherman sheath. If rain is predicted carry an umbrella, which can also be used for self-defence. Smearing yourself in sun block and walking around dressed as if you are about to climb Kilimanjaro only makes you stand out, this is a city, not the Serengeti

5. Find a fresh produce market. There will be food on sale, both cooked and raw, that you have never seen before. Experiment with a few, chat to the grocers, and buy some fruit to snack on back at the hostel

6. Eat where the locals eat. If there are two restaurants or two street food stands selling the same food, stand in the queue of the most popular proprietor. You will have to wait a little longer but you will get fresh, crisp food which should not give you the runs. Feel sorry for the other guy, buy a cool drink from them if you must, but do not eat their food if no-one else is

7. By eating what the locals eat, where the locals eat, you will gain a better understanding of the local culture and you will pay local prices. Hopefully you will enjoy the food. The most common and cheapest ingredients available will form the basis of the local diet. You can use these same ingredients in recipes which better suit your palette when you start cooking your own food

8. Try the local booze, beer and wine. You will want to buy a few bottles, where the locals buy their booze, and take them back to the hostel where you can usually refrigerate and drink them at your leisure in the communal area. Do not get drunk in public unless you are a skilled and controlled drinker. Getting buzzed in a hostel is usually great fun, there are people from all around the world who have travelled very far to have two weeks of fun. Party with them until they decide to hit the local nightclub, this is when you say "Sure, meet you there", then sneak off to bed. Next morning, they will be like, "where were you, man" and you will be like, "no way, I got lost". You will have a slight hangover, they will be green in the gills, slowly sipping water. You are a long-termer; night clubs are verboten!

9. Over weekends seek out flea markets and street malls. There will be street musicians and food stalls and artisanal brewery stalls. There will be hippies and little old ladies selling shoes and knitted goods, there will be the sights and sounds of the local artistic community

10. You can do all of the above with a partner or a family, they just need to be on the same page (remember to have your significant other study this book in the advanced stages of the Travel Indoctrination Campaign). Children are awesome travel companions if you have raised them well, they can walk for hours if they are motivated and interested and they look forward to trying new sweet foods and snacks. As the man of the house, I always walk behind my family as we explore cities or towns, you want to keep an eye on your flock and remember to do a regular head count if you are French. Let the kids carry a backpack each (local kids will also be carrying their school backpacks), this way they can carry jackets and snacks as well as the valuables (camera, credit cards, passports and a small amount of cash), which no-one will suspect if you are discreet and you get to keep an eye on them both

11. Having kids does not mean that you can't let your hair down. Ensure that you book into a safe, family friendly hostel if possible, remembering that any decent hostel will have an eye on security at all times, allowing only registered, paying guests and trusted friends to enter the premises. Your kids, depending on their ages, should be able to happily sit and watch a movie on a tablet or play a game while you have a few beers. Other travellers,

especially young pretty Scandinavian girls, love travel kids and will also keep an eye on your children, do not get distracted, family man. People trust a man travelling with a family and will treat you well

12. If you are a single man, travelling alone, expect people to treat you with a degree of suspicion, especially women. Single men are often suspected of having ulterior motives. The older you are the weirder they expect you to be. Do not undress people with your eyes, do not strike up awkwardly friendly conversations with the Scandinavian girls or the hostel receptionist. If you are going to the beach on your own, ignore the pretty sunbathing girls, do not act pervy, do not take photos of them sunbathing while pretending to read a book on your Smart phone. No one wants to play volleyball with your hairy, plump ass, let the young be young and frivolous, act your age. With any luck there will be a single lady traveller of your age sharing the hostel who would like to go wine tasting or for a walk to the park or street market or a museum. Enjoy her company, be a gentleman. Sex tourism is for dirty old men who chain smoke and talk too much

13. If you are a young single man, feel free to do whatever you want, within reason. The girls want you to chat to them, they want to have fun, their boyfriends are back home studying and even though they promised to be faithful they probably have no intention of following through. Be cool, be friendly, do not be a dick

14. If you intend to be in one region with a shared language for a long period of time, these first few weeks are a great period in which to do a language course, which will serve you well. The trick to speaking a new language is to immerse yourself in it fully. Use new words every day and look up the words which you are lacking. When speaking the language to locals do so in a very relaxed, almost lazy manner, they will assume that you are comfortable with the language and are an experienced traveller. If the conversation leaves you behind you should smile and go with the flow until something is said that you understand then agree or disagree. Read body language to fill in the gaps. You can use the same technique when talking to people who speak your language but say intellectual things which you don't understand.

You will need to do some preparation for your first few days as an Intercontinental Overlander:

1. Use your down time to research your overland route and border procedures, familiarise yourself with the terrain and bug the hell out of your local shipping agent. There are websites which track the progress of all RORO and container ships. Check these sites daily

2. Visit the local shipping agent and ensure that all the paper work is in order, familiarise yourself with the local port and establish the procedure for clearing your vehicle from customs

3. In all likelihood, it will take an entire day or two to clear the vehicle and it will probably be too late to leave the city on the day the rig is released from the port. Find a safe parking area where you can leave the vehicle for that first night

4. Plan the route to be driven from the port to a gas station and then to the overnight parking area

5. Be prepared for delays. The container containing your rig may be at the bottom of a huge pile, there may be a workers strike at the port, the weather may be too bad for off-loading, it may be a religious holiday or there might be a soccer match on TV. Being flexible is vital, realise that you are able to control only what you are responsible for

6. Eventually the email will arrive in your inbox or you will receive that much awaited phone call. "Let's go!" If your agent is worth his salt, he will speak English and will have a runner to do all the paperwork and running around. If not, you will need to pay careful attention to the procedures and insist on the process being done properly. If the customs procedure is not completed correctly you may encounter problems when leaving the country. Note, there is a separate chapter dedicated to the entire vehicle shipping process
7. Have your paperwork organised in order of importance
8. Be friendly and courteous with your agent and the customs officials, even if you desperately want to slap them with a wet fish
9. Ensure that you have photo copies of each document as well as a copy of your passport bio page and a copy of your entrance stamp
10. Having researched any fees payable as part of the process, ensure that you have sufficient amounts of local currency and US dollars on hand. Insist on a receipt for all fees paid
11. Try to contain your excitement as you walk through the port towards the waiting container
12. The customs seals should still be on the locked container doors and the keys to the rig in your hand
13. They might insist that someone else drive the vehicle or they might allow you to retrieve it. If someone else is to drive the vehicle out, hand them the ignition key and immobiliser and try to be present when they open the container. This does not apply to RORO, of course
14. This is the moment you have been waiting for. That first sight of your beloved rig on foreign soil is enough to give you goose bumps. With any luck the rig will be exactly as she was when you drove her into the container or onto the ship. Take photos with the agent and you and the rig, the rig and you and the customs guys, you and the rig and your family and the port workers. This is a big day in your life, you have achieved what very few others have done before you
15. Inspect the vehicle with the customs agent, complete the final paperwork, try to stay calm and breathe normally
16. With the temporary import papers completed and stamped in duplicate, you will be handed your copy and will be shown to the gate where your paperwork will be inspected and stamped
17. Different ports have different procedures but the above is pretty much standard practice around the world. There may be other inspections required by the traffic authorities, narcotics offices or agricultural inspections
18. With a lump in your throat and a rapid pulse you will complete the final bureaucratic hurdles and will be released onto the streets of the city
19. Fist pump, woohoo, let's do this baby, yee hah, damn I need a beer. Hell yeah!
20. More than likely you will need to put fuel in the gas tank as the customs agents back home had insisted that the vehicle hold almost no fuel before loading
21. Fill the tank and hand over a pile of cash, check the tyre pressures, oil and coolant
22. Drive through the streets with a big fat grin on your face, window open, waving at the common people
23. Park the vehicle at the overnight parking, double checking that everything is locked, take a few photos, check again that everything is locked, have a serious discussion with the security guard, explain to him how much you love your baby, make promises of large cash rewards should she be unmolested during the night. Check that she is locked one last time
24. Return to your hostel and have a few beers, upload the photos to the internet, try not to

have too many beers, eat dinner, go to bed. Tomorrow is the beginning.

It is tomorrow.

Wake up, regret your lack of restraint. Wonder if the rig made it through the night. Pack up, kiss all your new friends goodbye, hook up on Facebook. Promise to return or meet up somewhere on the planet. Arrive at the parking, the rig is sitting impatiently, wagging her tail. It's time to go, make your way through the city streets desperately trying not to break any rules of the road. High rises give way to apartment blocks which give way to houses, a freeway, an industrial area, you try not to miss your exit, your nerves are on edge and the hangover is not helping. You make it onto the road you will be following for the next few hundred kilometres, you curse the locals for driving like idiots, a long day passes behind the wheel, you begin to relax, just a little, you keep an eye on the fuel gauge and temperature gauge. Your GPS says turn right, you drive into the first little town, time to stock up on food, water and beer.

Your first night overlanding in a foreign country in your own vehicle is a truly unforgettable experience. All of those months, or even years, of hard work and single minded determination have paid off and here you sit, breathing fresh foreign air, an entire region, country or continent to explore.

Planning The Route

There are three styles of travelling

1. European Style

    I have German ancestors who I love dearly perhaps because they have no time for nonsense and their bullshit detectors are always set on full strength. They believe in hard work, discipline and perseverance, but, above all, they believe in order. There is a time and place for everything and a structure to order the day.

    Travelling in the European Style, is to explore according to a well-considered plan, which will balance the priorities of travel. One simply cannot visit every national park and tourist attraction; it would be foolhardy to try. Best is a systematic route focusing on the path of least resistance and those routes which offer the maximum percentage of reward for effort spent. The benefits of one couple finding another, perhaps Swiss, couple to travel with, will outweigh the negatives of convoy travel as there will be safety in numbers, companionship and shared cooking duties. Of course, one needs to retain order, the weeks and days shall not be allowed to flow into each other seamlessly. Time must be utilised efficiently, what works at home works best on the road. The week shall begin on Monday and the route planned to fit within a schedule of five days travelling and two days' rest. Friday nights there shall be a small party and a bottle of wine will be opened and perhaps a piece of meat consumed. Saturday shall be a day of shopping for supplies , spring cleaning and routine maintenance of the vehicle. Saturday evening shall be relaxed, perhaps social and Sunday will be spent reading a book, corresponding with family and friends back home and planning the route for the following week. Bed time is 10 PM throughout the week and

11pm on Friday and Saturday. Meals are to be determined by a set menu, breakfast of fruit, yoghurt and muesli, lunch of salad sandwiches and dinner as per the rotating schedule. On Wednesday nights, facilities permitting, a local meal will be enjoyed. Lists are very, very important. The cultural experiences one seeks shall be beneficial and cost effective with a goal of relevant self-improvement particularly in the understanding of language, geo politics, history and geography. The last weekend of every month will be spent in a comfortable yet affordable and highly recommended Bed and Breakfast where the month will be reviewed and the schedule adapted accordingly. There is no point in not learning from ones mistakes and adapting, ever so slightly if the planning was punctilious, or as required if incorrect. Within six months the bi-annual goals of the journey will be reviewed and the one-year plan will be updated. The end of year will be celebrated with family at home where presents bought in accordance with the list of expenses and responsibilities, with a particular effort made to ensure impartiality, shall be distributed. Over indulgence is permissible over the festive season.

2. African Style

There may be European blood in these veins but the body was born and raised on the sweet red soil of Africa. South of the Sahara, the continent sways to the beat of another drum, rhythmic and sensual. Africa is more than a beautifully shaped chunk of land, it is the birthplace of all humanity, we are all African, no matter the colour of our skin. The African style of travel is governed by the restrictions of African time which is fluid and does not conform to any clock. It is time to eat when a man is hungry and time to rest when the belly is full. Trying to control time is to attempt to control the ocean and the ocean obeys only the wind and moon. Life itself is a force and life will take you where it wants, your job is to listen to the voices on the breeze, flow with your emotions and embrace that which brings you closer to your love and peace. Each day will decide for itself where it wants to lead you, the people you meet and the experiences you have will be determined by the vibrations of the day. Some days the storms will come, dark clouds will crowd your head and thick, soft raindrops will cover your body in the life blood of the planet. If the Earth has anger, she will whip at you with winds and ice, she will remind you that you are but one of her creatures and the spirits will howl your name. If the Earth is pleased she will bathe your skin in sunlight and present you with the bounties of the land. Listen to the Mother Earth and follow where she leads you. She will speak to you in your dreams and quietly enter your thoughts, leading you, guiding you, teaching you what you need to know and taking you only where you need to be. Your reward will be a great wisdom, a journey of love and strength and power and beauty. Allow yourself to be free, allow yourself to be a child of the earth, allow yourself to embrace the uncertain, always knowing that tomorrow is another day and today will be but a memory, a ghost to flit on the wind, an ancestor of the man you are today. It is modern man who made time, in his suit and world of metal and concrete and glass, his technology and his politics and his wealth. He does not know his children, he does not listen to the earth, he does not free his spirit and trust tomorrow will be good if he has been good to today. The modern man lives by time and schedule, in fear of the future, working his whole life for his future only to find that when the future comes, he has not lived his life. African time is the stars in the sky, the strumming of the guitar, the laughter of the children, the love of a good woman. African time is time lived longer, more hours in the day, more pleasure in the night. African time is a bird on the wing, floating on the breeze, living free. Don't worry about a thing, coz every little thing, gonna be alright. (Of course, this is a generalisation. Modern Africa has super highways, sky scrapers, high speed trains, 4G internet and a few of the fastest growing economies on the planet).

3. The Veteran Overlander Style

The Veteran Overlander style of travel is a combination of two extremes. Planning and organization will ensure that goals are accomplished and that the journey is productive and less frustrating. Being open to new experiences and being flexible will ensure that you do not become disappointed by inflexibility and a rigid schedule.

We believe that balance is the key to a rewarding journey. If an overland journey is merely a checklist of guide book highlights, then a great opportunity has been lost. By getting off the major routes you will have an opportunity to meet locals who do have not have careers based on the tourist dollar and you will be able to have an authentic travel experience. Naturally, travelling far from major tourist routes is more demanding as the lack of organised camp sites and tourist facilities will force you to be more creative in finding a good, safe place to lay your -head, food and diversions.

There are three types of camping... Wild Camping, Free Camping and Paid Camping.

Wild Camping

Wild camping is usually a great way to save money when on the road. For instance, in Northern Brazil, which is sparsely populated outside the cities, we found that we could drive for very long distances on the beach. We would camp at night on the deserted beach as high as possible above the high water mark. We would make fires using coconut husks and old palm fronds, we would swim in the sea and do some fishing then fall asleep to the sound of the waves. We felt safe because we were so far from any humanity; our primary concern was a spring or extreme tide which could destroy the vehicle. We attached the winch cable to the nearest palm tree and connected the winch power lead in case of an emergency in the dead of night.

Wild camping could also fall under Paid Camping, depending on the circumstances of where you are but, as the name suggests, Wild Camping is essentially camping in the outdoors usually without any facilities such as ablutions or washing areas. Most likely you will pay to enter a National Park which allows camping in designated areas where you can camp or you will be in the middle of nowhere where Wild Camping is the only option. There are, naturally, extremes such as the notorious Canning Stock route in Australia where self-sufficiency is absolutely essential and a minor breakdown could have severe consequences. In this ever shrinking world it is difficult to find areas that remote. You will still find challenging terrain though, if you are prepared to go looking for it, and it is important to be mentally and logistically prepared.

- You may have to dig a hole for relief (always remember to dig the hole at least 30 cm's deep and ensure that all toilet paper is properly buried before moving on)

- Be self-sufficient for food, water and fuel. If there is an ocean or river nearby, you can wash and clean yourself, the water you carry on the vehicle should be reserved for drinking, cooking and brushing teeth
- Bathing every day is a luxury. Use wet wipes to freshen up the bits and change your undies daily. You will not smell your companions and they will not smell you. However, the first people you meet back in civilization will smell you for sure
- Saving water is very important, you do not want to run out in the middle of nowhere. This is why we are not great fans of those portable showers
- Travel responsibly, do not leave your litter behind, do not drive off established tracks where fauna or flora may be damaged, do not make or cause large fires, respect fellow travellers and leave only your footprints behind. Yes, I know, it sounds like a Nanny state but there is nothing more irritating than an inconsiderate traveller who treats nature (and fellow travellers) as something which needs to be dominated aggressively. Loud music is hated by everyone except the dick playing it. Bright lights are unnecessary, heavy drinking and disruptive drunken behaviour is just plain pathetic. Do not be a dick. I will give you an example. We read a story in a South African 4x4 magazine about a family who had travelled to a national park in Namibia. They had booked a semi wild campsite and arrived to find that a group of large bellied drunk people had drained the water tank (in a semi-arid area) to fill a portable inflatable swimming pool. These fat bellied buggers, drank all day and played loud, horrible music late into the night. If that is your idea of a good time I suggest you stay at home, sell the 4x4 and invest in an education. NB, I may be fat bellied and thirsty but I am also immensely considerate unless provoked, aren't we all
- Your vehicle must be reliable and equipped with emergency spares and sufficient provisions including fuel and medical supplies.

Free Camping

Free Camping is the budget overlanders best friend (or worst enemy, particularly if undertaken recklessly in a dangerous area). The average paid campsite will cost about $15.00 USD a night. If you intend to be on the road for an extended period of time you might want to consider Free Camping as often as possible. Having a "sleep in" camper will enable you free camp in many more locations than if travelling with a ground or roof top tent as you will be more secure. The best type of sleep in camper is the type which has free and open access from the living area to the drivers' cab, allowing a quick escape if the vehicle is under threat. Often Free Camping will be done in urban and semi urban areas and it is very important that overlanders are very careful to choose safe free camping and, if possible, seek the permission of the property or land owner/manager before settling in for the night.

Here is a scenario... you have been driving all day and you enter a highway system on the outskirts of a city which you do not intend to enter. You are far from the traditional tourist routes and your GPS does not show any options for camping, only inner city hostels, hotels and motels. The sun is setting and you are wary of driving at night. Your GPS does show that there are a number of gas stations on the perimeter of the city and long stretches of nothing thereafter. Your best option is to look for a gas station which caters to long distance truckers where you will find 24-hour security and toilets, perhaps even showers and a restaurant. Ask the attendants if you can park and sleep for the night then will leave in the morning after filling

up with gas. 99 times out of 100 they will oblige. Here are some gas station Free Camping tips:

- Assess the safety of the parking area. If there are shady looking characters, prostitutes and drunks present, you may want to move on
- Try to park away from trucks. In many countries drivers will idle the trucks engine throughout the night so that they can sleep with the air conditioning or heater on. There is nothing worse than spending a night breathing carbon monoxide. Truckers also keep weird hours and will arrive at the parking in the early hours or leave loudly at 3 am
- Be friendly with the presentable truck drivers, they also love the road, some even travel with a wife and children
- Keep a low profile but do not park in a dark corner where criminals might harass you
- Take advantage of the truck stop facilities. You may find a car wash, air for your tyres, clean water for your water tank, a spares store to top up on oil and other vehicle related provisions, a tyre repair service or windscreen repair
- If you make dinner, ask the security guard if he would like a plate of food. He will reward your generosity by keeping an eye on your rig while you sleep
- The parking area will usually be quite oily, watch your step
- Grab a cup of coffee and hit the road early, stop somewhere rural, pleasant and pretty for breakfast.

Other Free Camping options may include...
- A town plaza
- The parking area of a tourist attraction
- Outside a tourist or information office
- In the garden or driveway of a trusted new friend or acquaintance
- In the parking lot of a 24-hour store such as Walmart (actually a great place to free camp, you can buy a pizza and flat screen TV at 3AM)
- Hospital parking lots
- Almost anywhere well-lit and safe which does not have a Do Not Camp sign
- Outside a police station or military barracks, with permission
- In the grounds of a church
- In designated Free Camping areas (i.e., along the freeway in Argentina there are designated pull off camping areas)
- On the grounds of community sports and recreation areas
- In restaurant parking lots
- Public parks
- In a mechanics' yard
- On a soccer field in the middle of a village
- On Bureau of Land Management land in the USA
- On the banks of a lake or river.

NB, always remember to seek permission to free camp on private property and, as always, treat the locals with respect.

As you can see, the possibilities are endless, particularly if you have a sleep in vehicle. We have been able to free camp in all of the above places in a roof top tent, with two children, but we are always very cautious about where we camp. The one advantage we have is that Luisa sleeps very lightly and will awake to any strange noise, which makes for a bad night's sleep for her. She does get to catch up on her sleep while I drive the next day. Cyclists and bikers and those who use ground tents will have a much harder time finding free camping than those who travel in vehicles. Many cyclists find a spot next to the road and pitch their tent. The advantage the two wheeled people have is that their bikes are easy to hide and they do not need a large level area.

Paid Camping

Generally, we like to free or wild camp for five days then pay camp for two days, depending on the facilities available. This is a good time to get the laundry done, catch up with the processing of photos, catching up with friends and family on social media, taking care of emails, planning the route forward, having a braai with a bunch of friends and working on a hangover. Having saved so much money by free and wild camping during the week we are able to stay in highly recommended camps with great facilities, facilities which may include...

- Wi-Fi
- A games or TV room
- A laundry
- Hot showers and other indoor plumbing
- A swimming pool
- Green lawns
- Other members of the overlanding tribe
- Electricity
- BBQ areas
- A playground
- A restaurant and a pub.

If you find a camp with all of the above features at a good price, then you are in luck. You might even consider setting up camp for a week or so. I have a friend who calls this the overlanders disease and we have all fallen ill at one time or another. Ground tenters and roof top tenters particularly love a good established camp where you can hang out for a week or two recharging the battery. A good cheap campground is also a good place to do running repairs and maintenance of the vehicle. Take care not to kill the grass with old engine oil or soil the laundry basins by cleaning car parts. Be a considerate traveller. That includes not making fires and letting the smoke blow into your neighbour's rig. A South African can take it, we get hungry when we smell a forest or bush fire, but for many Europeans fire smoke is a complete nuisance. Lesson learnt.

If you do decide to stay for longer than a couple of days, negotiate a new rate for camping, often you will be able to get a full week for the same price as a few days. Remember:
- It is almost universal that children under 12 stay free and children under 16 pay half price
- If you do not need to hook up to electricity or water you should pay less
- Many camps in developing nations do not have card facilities so remember to carry sufficient cash

- Many countries have some type of tourist accommodation loyalty card such as Hostelling International or Good Sam or National Parks cards. By buying these cards you will be able to save significant amounts on reservations, entrance fees and accommodation. The longer you stay in one area, the greater the potential savings. If you are leaving a country and will never again use a loyalty card still valid for a few months, trade it with a nice tribe member heading the other way.

Hostels sometimes offer paid camping and are a great place to meet other travellers. Beware hostel camping. The backpackers and short term travellers have only a few weeks to have the time of their lives. They want to party, hard. And you, being a cool long-term overlander, are exactly the type of person they want to party with. Do not be surprised if a quick beer with dinner at the shared kitchen turns into a fire burning, rum swigging all-nighter. Good times.

When planning your route, you will need to carefully consider where you will be spending your nights.

Border crossings

Those of you who know us personally, will know that we, in that previous life, ran our own Immigration firm in South Africa. We kept the business small, specialised and highly competitive. Apart from being a very good business it also taught us many things. Perhaps the most valuable skill we learnt was how to effectively deal with bureaucracy, particularly the pesky third world bureaucracy which has its own nuances and requirements. In a developed nation, the immigration official is likely to be officious but efficient, his or her priority is to ascertain whether you have sufficient funds, no links with Al Qaeda and a valid visa. A third world (or the more politically correct term - Developing Nation) border official has the same requirements but sometimes a far less formal or efficient system for achieving the same result. The official may be bored, tired, under paid and under qualified with absolutely zero ability to self-motivate. **Typically, generalizations do not lend themselves to constructive discussion**, many borders are actually efficiently staffed, but let us assume that you are going to encounter the very worst type of border and border official and plan a strategy for working with them specifically, that way when you encounter efficient officials you will be pleasantly surprised but prepared nonetheless.

1. Have your ducks in a row

It is better to have too much documentation than too little. In most cases you will not have to present any back up documentation but if you are asked you want to be prepared.

- Research the visa requirements and establish what are your nationalities requirements before you leave for the border
- Ask travellers heading the other way about procedures and fees and spend some time researching the crossing on the internet
- Your valid passport, and those of your companions, should be kept in a plastic folder. Have duplicate or second passports stored separately. It helps to prepare all of your paperwork the evening before an intended border crossing

- Keep old or full passports handy, if you had previously and recently used them in the region you are travelling, you may be asked to show proof of an earlier entry or departure
- Also included in the folder should be two black ink ballpoint pens and any paperwork completed when entering the country such as a tourist information card. When entering a country overland, or by any other means of transport, you may have to complete a form which includes information such as name, date of birth, profession, country of birth and residence, destination within the country entering, desired period of stay, purpose of visit, declaration of compliance with foreign exchange limitations and declaration of compliance with agricultural regulations. Each individual will need to complete and sign a corresponding form, including children. NB, before eventually leaving the immigration office, try and secure a few of the corresponding forms which need to be completed when departing that country, you can complete these during your pre-crossing evening prep and will save time searching for the documents and a pen and perhaps losing your place in line
- Unless you are intending to take up employment in the country you are travelling to, keep your listed profession simple. So, if you're a Civil Engineer, you now become an Engineer, if you're Neuroscientist, you now become a Scientist. If you're a traveller by profession, you now become a Language Professor. Keep it simple but not too simple. They want professionals visiting, not long-term travellers who might try and find work and/or overstay their visa
- The folder should also contain certified original copies of birth certificates, marriage certificates and identification with the originals of those documents available for reference
- Be sure to carry up to date vaccination booklets for each individual
- Have valid credit cards available as proof of funds. Towards the end of your journey those credit cards may all be deeply in the red but there is no way for the common border official to establish the balance of your credit cards without a lengthy investigation which they have no interest in doing unless you are flagged for some reason
- Have your original vehicle documentation ready for inspection, you will need this documentation for the Temporary Import Permit or TIP which will be issued separately by customs once you have completed the immigration process
- If you are required to carry a carnet, make sure that you are stamped out of each country prior to entering the next one. Customs will not allow you to pass without proof of exit
- Some countries may require you to have your country sticker on your vehicle as well as different reflective tapes
- Some border crossings – we have yet to experience this, will require you to show a return ticket for your departure, even though you are entering by land – try FlyOnward.com to rent a ticket. It is temporary and will serve as sufficient proof to enter the country
- Photo copies. It is advisable to carry copies of the bio page of each passport and perhaps a copy of each entry stamp when departing the country. You may also need to provide copies of the vehicle documentation. In many cases the border officials will have a copy machine but that is usually for office use only, you may need to run to the little (but expensive) copy shop down the road which also sells vehicle insurance and Coca Cola.

The Border Procedure

Again, let us assume **a worst case scenario**. In our experience the most officious and difficult border crossings are those into and out of countries with a British colonial history, don't ask why, we don't know. Upon arrival at the border you will need to find safe parking and politely but firmly deny the services of the money changes and touts who offer to take your paperwork and walk you through the process. The border official waiting to ruin your day will be grossly overweight and very, very disinterested. He or she has just returned from their morning tea and are counting the minutes to an early lunch. Their uniform will be complimented with cheap, sparkling jewellery and their desk will be a mountain of paperwork weighted by a plate of various snacks. This official perhaps has an overbearing spouse and a den full of children but at the desk, armed with years of tedious experience and a stamp, they are in a position of power. But, first you will need to negotiate the crowds and queues of people jostling for their turn to be processed. Chances are it is very hot and humid, there is very little ventilation, the portly man behind you insists on rubbing his belly against your back and the snotty child staring at you over his mother's shoulder keeps sneezing and coughing into your limited personal space. The queue is separated by a soldier or uniformed guard, barking instructions in his language and doing so with no apparent adherence to a system:

- Stay calm and be patient, DO NOT expect the efficiency of your home nation
- Do not let people cut in front of you and feel no compassion for people carrying babies or little old ladies who ask to be allowed to go ahead of you, they will stop smiling as soon as they are in front of you then whistle for the spouse and ten kids to join them
- At the same time do what you can to get to the counter faster. If you have a travel companion have them stand in the other queue (the other queue always moves faster), place bets who will get to the counter first, swop queues when the first arrives at the counter and is attended to
- If there is no queue or system, just a mass of humanity slowly inching forward, belly to back, have your female companion elbow to the front saying "I just want to ask a question, excuse me, thank you, I just want to ask a question, excuse me, thank you". Do not make eye contact with anyone. When she gets to the front she will either be rebuffed or the official will ask for her passport, this is your cue to cut through the queue, dragging your kids along if you have, ignoring the protestations. "Sorry, she called me, thank you, sorry she called me, thank you". Do not speak in the local language, make up a language if you have to
- Once face to face with the official smile and be friendly
- DO NOT show anger or frustration, DO NOT complain to the official about the terrible process, DO NOT become impatient with the official when they ask a bunch of stupid questions, smile, be calm, explain what needs to be explained
- If the official explains that your passport is green not red and that your picture looks like an old woman, not you and that you need to return to the country you just came from to obtain a BI10006 form, DO NOT leave the counter, DO NOT argue loudly. Commiserate; they feel that they are suffering more than you are. They are just doing their job, and they are doing it well, thank them for their attention to detail. Explain that your companion nags a lot and has made you age before your time, explain that you made a phone call to the immigration office in his Capital city to confirm that the green passport is permissible and

you spoke to Janet, Janet said it was not a problem and that you would automatically be given 90 days upon entry. Of course, Janet does not exist but the official does not know that. If they say, "there is no Janet at Head Office", you will say, "maybe her name was Charlotte, I know her surname was Jenkins, anyway, she confirmed it and we double checked, could you confirm?". You are bluffing of course, but having done your research before entering the country you will know that you have every right to enter the country with your travel document

- Ignore the angry murmuring from the crowd behind you, do not leave the counter, ask the official to ask their superior
- You may have to do all of this communication in a combination of languages and using hand gestures
- Leaving the counter will not resolve your issue and will put you at the back of the queue, stay where you are, remain calm and polite
- The official will now either give in and stamp your passport or they might feel the need to save face in which case they will take your passport with them to another room where they will have a cup of coffee and kill some time flirting with a colleague in bright shoes and a tight uniform
- Ignore the stares from the crowd burning holes in the back of your head, chat quietly to your companion about a Plan B. Plan B will be to return to the rig, check that the tyres are still attached to the vehicle, and return to the office at lunch time when another official is covering for the first official
- Always ask for the maximum period permit for a tourist from your country unless you are specifically transiting through the country. You might have an emergency or a breakdown and need to stay longer in the country than anticipated. You might even fall in love with the country and decide to explore for a while longer
- Pay any fees which should be clearly listed and insist on a receipt, you might need to pay in local currency which can be obtained from a money changer or an ATM, if you are lucky
- Retrieve the stamped passports, thank the official and leave quietly while avoiding eye contact with the crowds.

Customs procedures

Generally, the customs procedure is less daunting than immigration. Most people crossing land borders do so on foot, arriving and departing the border by bus or taxi. The customs officials are less harassed by the general public and are usually better trained and seemingly more intelligent than the immigration officials. One would assume this is due to governments investing more resources in any services which are connected to control and taxation of goods and services. The customs office is usually cleaner, quieter and better run and might even possess a fan or air conditioning.

- After queuing, present the customs official with your stamped passport, the title deed and registration papers for the vehicle and/or carnet if required
- Anticipate a request for copies of your documentation
- Remember to be friendly and polite
- Point out where your name is listed on the papers, the registration number, the license number, the colour, the Vehicle Identification Number, the make and year of manufacture

- The official will single finger tap the information into the database while discussing last night's soccer match with a colleague hidden behind a wall of paper
- While waiting for the official to input your vehicle information look at the posters hanging on the walls, you are looking for any poster declaring prohibited goods, maintain a poker face should you spot one of your possessions on the list
- The official will eventually either return the completed carnet or print three copies of the Temporary Import Permit and ask you to sign all the three and keep one
- The carnet page is divided into three sections, each perforated. The customs official will need to complete the bottom section and partially complete the middle section, then stamp all three. He will then tear off the bottom section and keep that for his records. The middle and top sections will need to be completed and stamped by the customs official when departing the country, he will then tear off the middle section and keep that for his records. The top section will remain in the carnet book for your records and for the reference of the following countries customs officials
- He or she may then ask to inspect the vehicle along with the agriculture or narcotics inspectors, needless to say you must never try to cross a border in possession of any illegal drugs, regardless of quantity or your dependency
- If asked show the official the VIN number on the vehicle chassis, they may also want to confirm the engine number
- The agricultural inspector, it may be the same official, will ask you if you have any forbidden fruits or plant material
- Having done prior research, you will know if there are food products which you are not allowed to carry into the country, often some raw foods are forbidden but are allowed if cooked
- Always have a "sacrificial lamb", if oranges or apples are forbidden carry an apple or an orange, if the official asks if you have any of the forbidden products and you say no, they are likely to search the vehicle. If you say yes and hand over the offending articles they will likely not search the vehicle extensively, sometimes they are just curious about the vehicle and want to have a look around, because they can
- Open your fridge or cooler box and food crates and let the official inspect and remove whatever is on the list, there is no point arguing over a banana or a packet of lamb chops
- When the officials are satisfied that you are "clean", you have been cleared to leave and are in possession of all passports and the TIP, head to the final checkpoint where a guard will inspect your passports and TIP and lift the boom
- Head to the nearest camp and crack a cold beer and celebrate a new country a new adventure and one less bloody border crossing to endure.

The worst border crossing we have ever experienced - Colombia to Venezuela, Maicao

MEDICAL

The First Aid Kit

A well-stocked first aid kit could save your life, of course, that is what it is ultimately there for. However, you are far more likely to use medicinal supplies and sundry for the treatment of everyday irritations and minor injuries than for splinting broken bones and stitching up gaping wounds. Sunburn, diarrhea, splinters, cuts and burns are your most frequent health complaints, touch wood. It is best to have two first aid kits, both readily available. The larger kit should contain emergency and back up products, the smaller should contain daily used products. Older and younger passengers may require specialised products. Cyclists and Bikers need only carry a few plasters, diarrhea pills, a large crucifix and a whistle.

The small daily first aid kit should contain...
- Band aids in all shapes and sizes
- Elastic wrap bandages – also works great on animals
- Antibacterial cream
- Cottonwool balls
- Surgical gloves
- Alcohol swabs
- Nausea and diarrhea pills
- Headache and pain pills
- Sunburn ointment
- Sun lotion
- Tweezers and scissors
- Antiseptic wash
- Thermometer
- A syringe or two (including needles if travelling through Africa)
- Sanitary pads and few tampons, excellent to stop heavy bleeding
- Antihistamines
- Duct tape can be used as a temporary bandage
- Malaria medication and Coartem treatment for Malarial areas
- A large, loud whistle.

The large first aid kit should contain...
- Bandages in various sizes
- Eye shield or pad
- Triangular bandage
- Cold and hot packs

- Surgical gloves
- Cough medicine
- Bone splint
- Neck brace
- EpiPen
- Superglue can be used to seal deep wounds which require stitches in emergency situations when no medical services are available
- Sealed syringes and needles. If you have to receive medical attention in areas where medical supplies are scarce it may be better to have the practitioner assisting you use your own sealed, sterile needles
- Antibacterial cream
- A basic first aid manual.

Before leaving for any long term journey it is advisable to do at least a basic first aid course. You will want to know how to assess and stabilise an injured person, perform the Heimlich manoeuvre and CPR.

A certain Biker still owes me the debt of lifelong servitude for dislodging that piece of prime Argentine steak which blocked his throat. 'I'm joking', 'sure dude, everyone knows you are a smart ass'. 'I'm joking' he repeats, this time with more urgency. 'Whatever, man'. 'I'm choking!' He splutters through a purple face. 'Ah, shit, why didn't you say so?'.

As always, prevention is better than cure. Take care of your health, drive carefully and try not to ever put yourself or others in a life threatening situation. A medical emergency in the wilderness or far from infrastructure could have dire consequences.

Medical research shows that a handshake has one of the highest rate of transfer for bacteria. So, either fist pump or do as we do, hand sanitise. We carry hand sanitiser or antibacterial wet wipes at all times and it is essential to develop the habit of either washing your hands with water or giving them a good wipe with the wet wipes before eating or putting hand to mouth.

Common Illnesses and Treatment

There are several ways to keep healthy while travelling besides eating healthy. When venturing to foreign lands you will be exposed to germs and bacteria which your body has not been in touch with before. I have compiled a list of common illnesses that either you or your children may experience along the way. We are not doctors and the information provided hereunder is from our experience or other's. We do not take any responsibility for any injuries, and it is vital that a professional opinion be sought in case of a severe wound or illness.

Allergies – Hay fever is not dangerous but more of an annoyance with sneezing, watery eyes and a runny or stuffy nose. Allergies to food can be more life threatening and should be treated as such. Carry antihistamines at all times and as a precautionary, get an EpiPen for anaphylaxis shock. And no, don't do a Pulp Fiction and stab it into the heart, it goes into the outer upper thigh, preferably. We've carried one for the past 7 years since our first trip in 2009 and although we have never had to use it (touch wood), some day, someone may.

Nausea and vomiting – This can be caused by a common flu or the dreaded travellers bug induced by dirty hands preparing your meal. You can either let the bacteria run its course and drink loads of fluid, excluding alcohol or you can take medicines that contain domperidone or dexamethasone. If you have motion sickness, try and get medication containing hyoscine, cinnarizine, cyclizine or promethazine.

Ear Infections – There are different parts of your ear which can become infected. The outer ear inflammation caused by water, dirt or debris entering the ear canal is generally referred to as swimmer's ear. Symptoms include itchiness, pain and warmth. The ear canal may also be swollen and you may experience pain when chewing. It will clear up on its own but it is recommended to use home remedies such as rinsing the ear with warm saline solution or half-half of water and white vinegar (I can attest to the latter). The middle ear generally becomes infected when germs from the common cold become trapped and cause an infection. When yellow pus or blood comes from the ear, it means the eardrum has burst and the pain and infection should subside in a few weeks. Try and keep the ear dry and do not submerge in water. When the inner ear gets swollen and inflamed from a viral infection or less commonly from a bacterial infection, you will experience several symptoms, i.e. vertigo, hearing loss or ringing in the ears. You can use an antibiotic containing penicillin to clear away most ear infections or you can also use a topical aesthetic drops to "deaden" the inflamed eardrum.

Conjunctivitis/Pinkeye – Tearing, redness, itchy and crusty eyeballs? Yip, that's pinkeye. It is annoying and fortunately does not generally require treatment. The bacteria usually spread because of poor hygiene and yes, it is contagious. Try not to share towels or shake hands. If you have viral pinkeye, this is from the herpes virus. You will have the same symptoms but with a white discharge. Keep it clean at all times.

Schistosomiasis/Bilharzia – This is a caused by a parasitic worm that comes from fresh water snails. Long story short but if an infected person urinates or defecates in a standing body of water, the eggs then swim off and breed in snails, they then leave the snails and penetrate your skin and you contract bilharzia. Our Jessica contracted Bilharzia after swimming in Lake Malawi. We were not aware of this as she only developed symptoms a few months after we returned to South Africa and after almost a year of regular doctor visits, several courses of antibiotics and a day before surgery was to take place, Graeme mentioned it might be Bilharzia, one dose of Praziquantel/Biltricide and it was all cleared up. Her bladder was free of the mass of eggs spawned by the pesky parasite.

Impetigo – Sores that form into blisters and is easily, and I mean VERY easily spread to other parts of the body and highly contagious. If you have an open wound, keep it clean and dry. Your skin infection, scratch or cut will take a longer time to heal in a warm, humid and tropical environment and you are more susceptible to impetigo or other skin infections. Use an iodine based cream for any cuts or scratches but please beware of using iodine on small children and adults that are prone to be allergic. When treating impetigo or multiple wounds remember to clean each wound individually, using clean materials and dressings for each.

Ringworm – This is not in fact caused by worms but rather by a fungus. It causes a red, scaly, itchy ring on the skin. This is also very contagious and is treatable via anti-fungal medication.

Strep throat – Symptom is a sore throat that lasts longer than a week, along with excessive drooling and pain when swallowing. This is not a common cold, this is caused by the strep bacteria and you will need antibiotics.

Rabies – If you get bitten by an animal or some human frothing at the mouth, chances are you will have to get a rabies shot. You can be vaccinated prior to your trip and this may slow down the parasites but if bitten, you will need a repeat shot or two.

Mosquitoes – I've given them their own category as they are a bloody nuisance and can cause several illnesses which can be deadly. If you can, take medication when in an area with dengue, yellow fever and malaria.

There are 5 types of medication:

Malarone (our preferred medication) – Daily oral doses required, a preventative as well as a treatment
Chloroquine – Weekly oral doses required, some mosquitoes are resistant to this drug
Doxycycline – Daily oral doses required, increased risk to sun sensitivity - which is not an option with freckles and fair skin
Mefloquine/Lariam – Weekly oral doses required, not recommended in people with psychiatric conditions, seizure disorders, cardiac problems
Primaquine – Effective in most areas, daily oral doses required, you must be tested for G6PD deficiency before use

In areas with known cases of Malaria it is important to take the necessary precautions to prevent being bitten...
- Identify the local risk. In parts of the Southern Hemisphere, Mother Nature tasks mosquitoes with killing us by various means - Zika, Dengue and Malaria in South America and a particularly nasty cerebral Malaria in Sub Saharan Africa (with the exclusion of Namibia, parts of Botswana and most of South Africa) which still kills a million people a year, mostly pregnant woman and children
- Wear long sleeve shirts and trousers from dusk, if possible. If too hot, use a repellent spray or cream
- Use mosquito nets, be sure to repair any holes in the netting and to keep the sleeping area sealed
- Regularly spray the tent, cabin and cab areas of your vehicle with DEET or similar effective spray. Mosquitoes love to hide behind the dashboard and under the seats and will feast on your legs as you drive
- Apply an effective repellent cream to exposed areas of flesh, including the neck, ears and even face if the vampires are bold and thirsty. There are various homeopathic ointments which have varying degrees of potency and effect. Unless you know for sure that your hippy ointment is going to repel the mosquitoes, do not take a chance, particularly in high risk areas. If you are looking for other natural remedies, oil of lemon eucalyptus will help

- The higher the altitude, the lower the probability of getting bitten
- Anti Malaria tablets can only be used for a limited amount of time, usually a few months, and the constant application of chemicals to your epidermis simply cannot be healthy
- Avoid camping near swamps or bodies of standing water, large or small
- Carry a battery operated tennis racket shaped mosquito zapper. The zapper electrocutes the little bastards and there are few things more satisfying than hearing the ZAP! of another perfectly executed execution. Revenge has never been more fun
- REMEMBER, mosquitoes do not only feed throughout the night but also in the mornings, do not let your guard down for the first few hours after sunrise

Symptoms of mosquito borne virus':

Malaria – chills, fever, sweating, diarrhea, nausea and vomiting. Is often mistaken for a hangover. Drink loads of fluids and get treatment quickly. The best on the road treatment is Coartem (Artemether/Lumefantrine) which you can buy before you leave.

Dengue Fever - nausea, headache, fever, vomiting, rash, pain in your joints, muscles and eyes. Drink loads of fluids and take analgesics for the pain and fever, severe cases may require hospitalisation. Coconut water is an excellent source of hydration which can be used in lieu of a saline drip if required.

Zika - mild fever and skin rash, usually accompanied by conjunctivitis, muscle or joint pain, and general malaise that begins 2-7 days after the bite of an infected mosquito. One out of four infected people develop symptoms of the disease. There's no vaccine or specific treatment. Instead the focus is on relieving symptoms and includes rest, re-hydration, and acetaminophen for fever and pain. Aspirin and non-steroidal anti-inflammatory drugs like ibuprofen should be avoided. Pregnant women should avoid travelling to areas where the Zika virus is endemic as a bite may result in microcephaly, a condition in which a baby's head is significantly smaller than expected.

The symptoms and treatment of other common maladies...

Yellow Fever - generally found in Africa and South America – causes nausea, fever, headache and yellow eyes and/or skin (jaundice). Drink plenty of fluids. You can be vaccinated against Yellow Fever and a vaccination certificate is required for the entry to many countries.

Typhoid Fever – Is serious and is a bacteria caused by contaminated food and water. You will experience high fever, weakness, headache and stomach pains. Rule of thumb to avoid this is to eat hot food, drink bottled water and wash your hands regularly. Drink loads of water and if necessary get a penicillin based antibiotic.

Hepatitis A and B – A is spread by contaminated food and water. It is a virus and you can be vaccinated against it. B is transmitted through blood, blood products and bodily fluids – easy one to avoid by using a condom, not getting tattoos with dirty needles, medical or dental procedures in unsterile environments and lastly not doing drugs!

Tetanus – Stepped on a rusty nail while looking for a part? Yes, it did happen and no I didn't die but I was vaccinated. If you get vaccinated you'll also be covered for whooping cough, just saying….

Diarrhea – By far the most common ailment suffered by travellers. It is almost guaranteed that you will experience a bout of diarrhea on your trip, if not then perhaps you are not being adventurous enough. There are many causes from spoiled or badly prepared food, that mature meat you bought from the local market or from bacteria passed on either through contact or otherwise ingested. You can let it run its course and keep taking in fluids if you are in a comfortable place with a private commode or you can put an end to it with any medicine containing loperamide or bismuth subsalicylate. If you're camping in a remote area with no access to a bathroom, best you medicate. Do not attempt to continue travelling until your stomach has settled completely. In South Africa we have a product called Imodium Melts which are tiny little pills which melt quickly in the mouth and offer rapid relief.

The following are common childhood diseases:

Chickenpox – Itchy, blistery, fever inducing chickenpox. It first appears as a rash on the stomach, back and face and then spreads like wildfire all over the body. Don't scratch. Put gloves on your kids hands if they do. Calamine lotion and antiviral medications work best.

Meningitis – Firstly, get vaccinated, this is the best option to avoid this disease. In case of infection you will experience a fever, headache and a stiff neck and can it also be presented as the flu in children. It is an inflammation or infection of the tissue around the brain and spinal cord, depending on the cause, meningitis may get better on its own, or it can be life-threatening, requiring urgent antibiotic treatment.

Mumps – Symptoms include swollen glands between the jaw and ear. Treatment focuses on symptom relief. Recovery takes about two weeks. The disease can be prevented by the MMR vaccine.

German measles/Rubella – A mild virus in children but can be dangerous to pregnant women. Can be avoided by vaccination.

Measles – Symptoms include runny nose, fever and cough. Can be avoided by vaccination however if unvaccinated it can clear up within a few weeks but can become more complicated.

Please remember that giving aspirin to children or teens is not advisable. If they have a viral illness, they may be prone to Reye's syndrome, which could lead to heart damage.

You'll notice that most childhood diseases can be avoided by vaccination. I believe it is a contentious issue amongst some folk but I believe prevention is better than a cure.

These are some vaccinations you should consider from birth to the age of 6 years:

Chickenpox	Diphtheria	Hib
Hepatitis A and B	Measles	Mumps

'Pertussis (whooping cough) Polio Pneumococcal
Rotavirus Rubella Tetanus

These vaccinations and booster shots should be taken in conjunction with the above at different ages from 6 years. You can speak to your local clinic or doctor about the relevant vaccinations:

Tetanus, Diphtheria, Pertussis HPV Meningcoccal
Pneumococcal Hepatitis A and B Polio
Measles, Mumps, Rubella Chickenpox

Again, we are not doctors and the information provided here is from our own personal experience. We do not take any responsibility for any injuries or misdiagnosis, it is vital that a professional opinion be sought in case of a severe wound or illness. Be smart, check your facts before taking any medicines or treatments.

BATHROOM BLUES

One of my nagging concerns before going on our first international overland journey in late 2009 was the daily dependence on communal bathrooms. I worried about unclean toilets, infections and diseases and I worried about communal showers. I am not generally shy but I prefer to do my bathing in private and I particularly did not want my children to bathe "publicly".

For those long-term travellers who do not have a vehicle with indoor plumbing, and perhaps even those who do, a realistic daily concern is public bathing and bowel evacuation. Yes, going to the loo. If you are one of those people who refuse to go No2 in a public restroom, you may struggle. Our little Jessica used to refuse to use a toilet which had even a stained bowl and refused to take a crouching bush pee until she was about 10 years old. This can not only be inconvenient in the middle of nowhere but can also be unhealthy for girls, leading to painful bladder infections.

The reality is that the smart phone in your hand carries more germs than the average toilet seat and you press that bacterial soup against your face every time you receive a call. Apologies, these are not the things one discusses in polite company but we shall in the interest of personal hygiene. This is our public ablution routine:

- The kids will wait until we have driven ten minutes from a nice clean gas station or camp and announce that they need the toilet
- We will ask them why the heck they didn't go when we asked them if they needed to eleven minutes before
- They will respond that they did not need to then but now they really, really do
- We will keep on driving, looking for a restaurant or another gas station
- Eventually, when the child has turned blue, we will find potential relief
- We will inspect the bathrooms and choose the cleanest cubicle
- We touch nothing with our bare hands, instead using toilet paper to open doors
- If the bathroom is particularly gross, we will wipe the seat (hopefully there is a seat) with disinfectant wet wipes and dry with toilet paper, remember to have a small pocket bag of wet wipes readily available
- If the bathroom is not disgusting we will just wipe the seat with paper, lay down a strip of toilet paper on either side of the seat and position our gluteus maximus perfectly on the strips and ensure that no other part of the anatomy makes actual contact with the seat
- For obvious reasons it is very important not to let your trousers or undies make contact with the floor, this can be achieved by folding them into themselves above the shoes or spreading your ankles until the fabric is taut
- Do your business while reading how much Alexander loves Juanita and appreciating his passion for poetry and the penis, large or small
- Using a clean piece of toilet paper to avoid contact with the handle, flush the toilet, unlatch and open the door
- If soap and running water is available, dispense and flip the tap on with the flick of a finger, wash, rinse, repeat
- Leave the bathroom while making an effort not to touch the door handle. Why do bathroom doors not swing open from the inside? Why can you push the bathroom door open when entering but have to turn a handle to leave?

- If there was no soap or running water clean your hands thoroughly with either a disinfectant wet wipe or waterless hand sanitiser.
- In remote areas we usually take a walk with a spade and a roll of toilet paper.
- Look for a quiet, private spot behind a tree or boulder
- Check the area for snakes, spiders, scorpions, centipedes or anything else which could harm you or ruin the moment
- Dig a hole at least thirty centimetres deep
- Squat using the spade for stability, lean back a bit and pull your under garments out of harms way
- The squat is actually the most natural position for executing bowel movements though hardly the most comfortable
- Drop used toilet paper into the hole and cover with the soil removed when digging the hole
- Wash your hands well

If the idea of squatting and dropping your delicates in the bush does not appeal to you, there are a few alternatives such as a small porta potti, a camping chair with a precut hole, a toilet seat attached to the rear bumper of your rig or a tall dedicated ablution tent. We have tried all of these other options and eventually settled on the good old spade.

Despite my initial fears, we have hardly ever encountered communal showers without private cubicles. Yes, there will probably be one of those horrible shower curtains which will blow up against your back and a spider or two might share the shower but you will, at least have privacy.

- Ladies, before entering a secluded communal shower ensure that there are no strangers lurking
- If there are multiple shower cubicles check the water pressure of each shower before choosing the one with the best pressure
- If possible remove the shower head if the water flow is too slow, often the shower head is blocked which will restrict the flow. Replace the head when finished
- Remember to always wear flip flops in the shower
- In areas with water shortages wet your body thoroughly, turn off the water, wash yourself from head to toe then turn the water back on and rinse
- Learn to embrace the cold shower. Hot water is a luxury and cold water showers are actually good for your blood circulation, besides, you will often be forced to have cold showers; you might as well enjoy it
- In cold climates it is often not necessary to shower daily. Rather use wet wipes for quick cleans and shower only when a decent, hot shower presents itself. A cold dribbling shower on an ice cold day is simply torture
- Keep toiletries in a waterproof bag with a hook for hanging. You will not believe how many campsites have showers with no hooks for hanging towels, clothing and toiletry bags
- The toiletry bag should only contain what you need daily
- Keep your soap in a little plastic soap box
- Check that you leave nothing behind when leaving the shower area
- Hang your towel to dry over the door of the vehicle, on a washing line or from a tree, try not to forget it when you leave camp.

Dealing with trash

A large chain supermarket recently launched a new and innovative idea which I am sure you have seen lambasted on the internet. In an effort to reduce food wastage, the executives decided to package oranges in a clear plastic container resembling a large version of the half dozen egg containers. Talk about redundancy. Unfortunately, you may find while overlanding that most of your trash is food packaging and much of that is plastic. Unfortunately many countries do not have the resources or infrastructure to recycle glass, aluminium, waste paper or plastic but there are many signs that that is starting to change, particularly in and around cities. Your challenge while travelling is to try to make as little negative impact as possible, on both the environment and the cultures you engage with. Often you will not find a decent receptacle for your trash and may have to carry it for long distances before finding a decent place to dump it.

- Never litter or carelessly dump plastics, ever
- Encourage others not to litter
- Try to minimize your waste generation by shopping wisely. 12 x 500ml bottles of fluid may be convenient but uses significantly more plastic than 3 x 2L bottles
- Where and when possible, purchase fruit and vegetables from farmers markets and don't be afraid to purchase your meat there as well (if the meat is fresh and not covered in flies, not only will you produce less garbage you will also help the local economy, engage directly with the locals and perhaps learn a few new words
- Use your own cloth shopping bags
- If you have a campfire and there are no recycling facilities available, burn all paper products in the fire, never plastic. A fire is not a dump
- Organic waste such as fruit or vegetable peels or skins, can be discarded wherever it will not cause inconvenience to others, the Earth's critters may thank you
- Use as few plastic bags as possible
- Crush cans underfoot and squeeze the air out of plastic bottles and, if possible, rinse both if you will need to store the trash in or on your rig for any length of time
- Invest in a strong bag for the storage of trash. There is a popular product called the Trasharoo which attaches to the rear spare wheel common on many 4x4s, alternatively use a dry bag lined with a thick rubbish bag
- Keep trash out of reach of animals. In Africa and Asia, monkeys can be a real problem, tearing up rubbish bags and stealing unattended food. In North America trash and unattended food can attract bears (who are also apparently obsessed with toothpaste).

Misc.
Tips

An improvised mixer

A 12 volt cordless drill is a handy tool, particularly if accompanied by a multitude of attachments for drilling and grinding. You could also use the drill for mixing dough, polenta and making scrambled eggs. Simply attach a single cake mixer blade as you would a drill bit and mix away. This also works great for mixing pots of paint.

Spare Key

I cannot remember how many times we have locked the keys in the Land Rover. Kids. We have had a few spare door and ignition keys made and have stashed a couple in secret hiding places in the body of the Land Rover which are accessible with a Leatherman tool. The keys are wrapped in plastic bags and duct tape to avoid rust and damage. If the keys are locked in the rig or in the sad event that the keys are lost, we are able to access the vehicle. No, I will not tell you where we hide the keys.

Hiding Money

As with the spare key it is often a good idea to hide some Dollars, Euros or Pounds somewhere on the vehicle. When we drove into Venezuela there was a significant concern that we might be robbed because as tourists we were guaranteed to be carrying US Dollars and, at that time, a Dollar was worth ten times the official rate on the black market. We were carrying $4000 and decided to put a quarter in the safe, a quarter in the roof tent, a quarter stashed behind the tail lights wrapped up in plastic and duct tape and a quarter spread around the cabin of the Defender. This way if we were ever robbed we would only lose half, maximum, unless they stole the entire vehicle.

Dealing with critters

When camped beneath trees, try to ensure that the branches do not touch the vehicle. Ants will use the tree to invade your roof top tent or camper and once in, are very difficult to remove. Also, in cold areas, critters (mice, rats and some marsupials) may climb into the engine bay of your vehicle to stay warm and, while there, may kill time chewing through your electrical cables and eating holes in the bonnet and firewall liner.

In areas with scorpions and large spiders it is advisable to keep shoes off the ground when not being worn, leave socks in the mouth of shoes to prevent the scorpions and spiders from getting in and never leave clothing lying on the floor, also be sure to check your shoes for invaders before putting them on. Give any garments a good shake before putting them on. The same applies to gathering wood, be careful how you pick it up, wear gloves if possible. When moving logs onto the fire, be sure to check the ends for scorpions who may have been clinging to a log and are now trying to escape the heat. Scorpions are luminescent under ultra violet light and a small UV torch will light them up like Christmas. The rule of thumb with scorpions is that those with large pincers and a small stinger are generally not extremely dangerous while those with small pincers and a large stinger are.

Spiders are usually scarier than they are dangerous unless you are in Australia in which case they are evil bastards who live only to kill you.

Snakes are mostly more interested in self preservation than in murder with a few exceptions particularly in Africa and Oz. Keep vehicle doors shut, do not leave large pieces of gear lying on the ground where snakes can find shade and be careful where you step. If you come face to fang with a snake, do not try to catch it even if it is relatively small; juvenile snakes dump venom when they bite so are just as dangerous as the adults. Back away slowly from the snake, making no fast movements and keeping eye contact. If approached, the Southern Africa Rinkhals snake acts dead by rolling on its back, mouth agape, it may even let you pick it up and play with it for two or three minutes before BAM it bites and you lose an arm or it sprays its venom in your eyes and you wish you were dead. Snakes tend to get underfoot in the mornings when they are slow and seeking sunshine to warm their cold blood.

Stray dogs can be either cute and cuddly or vicious and infected with rabies. Never put your face in a stray dogs face even if you have been rubbing it's tummy for an hour. Feed them scraps and maybe even carry a bag of dog food and a couple water bowls if you are an animal lover. Never adopt a stray unless you are heading directly home and have the budget for a massive expense. Cats are cats, they will do whatever the hell they want to.

When travelling in National Parks full of bears or lions or elephant or hyena obey the park instructions. Never feed wild animals, do not get out of the vehicle to take a better photo of the lion, you are not in a zoo. They will eat you.

Beer

Beer is the third most popular beverage on the planet. Only water and tea keep the amber fluid from its rightful position as king of drinks. Beer snobs will find imported and specialty beers in almost every city around the world, with the obvious exception of those countries where alcohol is forbidden. The average beer drinker will be happy with either a decent lager or pilsner which can be found in almost every small village, town or city. Zythology, the study of beer and beer making, has been undertaken for thousands of years. Egyptian workers apparently drank four litres a day while building the pyramids and Vikings believed that in Valhalla there is a giant goat whose udders provided an unlimited supply of beer. That settles it then, I chose Valhalla to while away eternity.

- When designing your overland rig be sure to have a storage area designated specifically for the storage of beer
- The beer storage area should be cool and easily accessible
- You want to be able to carry 24 cans because 12 is too few and cans travel better than bottles and are usually cheaper to purchase and easier to dispose of when empty
- The morning beer prep is an extremely important part of your day. You want to ensure that at least six cans of the golden goodness are allotted space in the fridge or cooler. At the end of a long drive you will want a few cold cans to wash away the day
- If drinking directly from the can be sure to rinse and wipe the mouth of the can to avoid ingesting bacteria
- Try as many of the local beers as you can before settling on a few to be your staple
- A can of beer wrapped in a wet cloth will cool rapidly in a cold fridge or freezer
- A wet cloth or a beer cozy will keep the nectar of the Gods cold while you drink it, I find that drinking a cold beer quickly and enthusiastically prevents it from getting warm
- Be sure to budget a proportionate amount of your travel kitty for the purchase of beer.

Wine

Buy a few bottles, store them in a cool place, drink them when you run out of beer. Do not run out of beer.

Online resources

IOverlander

iOverlander is a mapping project created to help overlanders on the road find their next destination. We are in two minds about using the app regularly and prefer to use it as a reference though it has proven to be very useful at times, particularly when we are struggling to find safe camping in urban areas while in transit. Others use the app almost exclusively, I suppose it depends on your style of travel. We recommend using the app specifically to those who are new to overlanding or are particularly social. iOverlander, as with everything in life, has its pros and cons...

Pros
- Up to date information on hand, (an excellent resource in emergency situations)
- Lists information on a variety of relevant elements including border crossing info, accommodation, military checkpoints, fuel supplies, medical, mechanical workshops, etc
- Free
- Easy to use
- Rateable by the user
- Contains reviews and opinions
- International
- User updated

Cons
- User updated
- Android compatible but is far more user friendly on the iPhone for which it was designed
- Reviews are not always viable, correct or usable, depends on travellers style
- "No secret spots", a great secluded camp, kept secret by the cool kids, once listed on iOverlander becomes a public camp. Not great if you are anti-social, hence an overlander
- The app has low "adventure" appeal

Maps

We initially used a Garmin Nuvi GPS, but it would first take us through the favella's (slums) in Brazil before driving into the city. We promptly threw it out shortly thereafter. We now use two android mapping systems namely, MapFactor Navigator and Google Maps. There are more options as follows:

- Maps.me
- Genius maps
- City Maps
- Guidepass
- Alltrack – walking trails for the USA
- Frommers ebook maps

There are the following GPS maps that can be used, some country or region specific:

- Argentina and Chile – Proyetcto Mapear.com.ar and Conosur

- Bolivia – Bolirut.com
- Brasil – tracksource.org.br
- Central America – Cenrut.org
- Colombia – ColRut.com
- Peru – perut.org
- Venezuela – Venrut
- Specific to Africa - Tracks4Africa
- Specific to Australia - 4x4earth
- OpenStreetMap – for all other countries not listed

Other Useful Applications
- WhatsApp – chat
- Hangouts - chat
- Duolingo – Teaching you a new language
- Google Translate
- Weatherunderground – accurate weather forecasting
- Flashlight phone
- Flipboard - news
- Zinio – online magazines

Working on the road

Take a look at some of these websites for some inspiration. Many are unfortunately IT specific but you could learn a new set of skills that will enable you to be "employable" whilst travelling:

Volunteer opportunities:

1. Workaway
2. WWOOF
3. Helpstay
4. Gooverseas.com – a paying portal
5. Helpx.net
6. Peacecorps.gov – only open to US citizens
7. Seaturtles.org
8. Kibbutzvolunteer.com – only in Israel
9. Unv.org
10. TheMuskokaFoundation
11. USO

Freelancer opportunities:

1. Freelancer.com
2. Freelance.com
3. Freedlanced.com
4. Guru.com
5. Fiverr.com

6. Peopleperhour.com
7. Upwork.com
8. Project4hire.com
9. TopTal
10. Freelancewriting.com

Seasonal or part-time work

1. PickingJobs.com
2. Needafarmer.com
3. Clubmedjobs.com
4. Backdoorjobs.com
5. Transitionsabroad.com
6. Seasonworkers.com

Or alternatively, you can complete an online TEFL/CELTA/TESL/TESOL course which will enable you to teach English as a Second Language. This might be a great opportunity for some singles or young couples to fill up the coffers. Just remember that it does not pay extremely well (so, not recommended for Family travellers) and if English is not your first language you may have a hard time securing a position.

There are massive amounts of resources and websites for teaching English, but be forewarned, there are a lot of corrupt agencies out there looking for their next sucker. The best resource we found when we were looking at teaching English after completing our TEFL course was Dave's ESL Café, www.eslcafe.com, I believe that it is the best resource out there.
The above are to name a few. There are many other resources available on the internet.

Where to sell your photos

Shutterstock
Dreamstime
Foap
DepositPhotos
StockFresh
Fotolia
iStock
BigStockPhoto

Websites, forums and other sources of information

The Internet is the modern overlanders greatest resource. In days of old, explorers would have to spend months doing research and corresponding with bureaucratic agencies before finally being sufficiently prepared for their wild drive from London to Singapore. These days you can find whatever information you need within minutes, particularly if you know where to look. Do not ever take this resource for granted. In this, the golden age of the Internet, we have free access to all of humanities combined intelligence and information, a freedom of information which we can now tap into but are not always guaranteed to have as various government agencies seek to control the free flow of ideas.

Here follows a few of our favourite resources:

Facebook pages
African Overlanders
PanAmerican Travelers
Overland Sphere
Expedition Portal
Land Rover Owners
A2AExpedition (the best by far)
On the road in Mexico
Talk Baja
Drive The Americas
International Overland Families
Horizons Unlimited Motorcycle Adventure Travellers
Land Rover Defender 90 110 130 Series Owners Club (a great place to pose technical questions)
BMW GS Adventures RTW
Offroad and Overland Expedition Vehicles

Forums/websites
Expedition Portal
Wikioverland
The 4x4 Community (Southern Africa)
Overland Sphere
A few other online resources
- Airbnb – rental accommodation
- Bookings.com – hotel accommodation
- Pimms – language lessons
- Anthony Bourdain – has a lot of country specific episodes for your culinary experience
- Lonely Planet ebooks
- Freecampsites.net

And of course, Wikipedia.

Food preparation & recipes

ROAD FOOD

After a couple of weeks on the road you should have a very good idea of which ingredients are available and which represent the best value in terms of cost and nutrition. It is very difficult to break old habits, particularly when it comes to something as daily and repetitive as food intake, but you will need to experiment with new dishes and methods of preparation. Depending of the remoteness of the route you plan to follow, it is best to buy groceries for the next two or three days only. Resist the urge to fill two shopping carts with groceries and cram it all into your little fridge and food crate.

This section aims to provide you with cooking tips and recipes which will save you money and help you achieve culinary greatness, or, at least, a full belly.

MAKING A FIRE

Have you managed to tap into that instinctual flare for fire making? This may be something that you want to practice before leaving home. No, you do not need the flint and striker survival fire starter unless you plan to get very far from civilization and do not plan to carry a couple of Bic lighters or a large box of matches. Here are a few fire making tips...

- When possible carry your own firewood and/or a large bag of charcoal. Most of the developing world has a close relationship with fire, particularly where an electricity or liquid gas infrastructure is not readily available
- Different types of wood burn differently. Dry hard wood burns the best and leaves high temperature, low smoke, long lasting coals. Good wood is a precious commodity and should be used sparingly. Light, wet wood burns terribly, creates a lot of smoke and produces weak coals. A bonfire is only good for large groups and special occasions
- Charcoal is most reliable and is usually light weight. Ensure that you have an empty space outside your rig for the storage of charcoal and wood, preferably in a large plastic bag if rain and heavy dew are likely.

Lighting a fire can often be difficult. Even real men struggle sometimes, they just won't ever admit it. Here are a few fire lighting tips and procedures.

- You will want to ensure that the fire is made within a designated area or an area which you have cleared. You do not want to allow sparks from the fire to ignite the surrounding area. Not only is this dangerous for you, your rig and crew, it is also very dangerous for the local fauna and flora as well as the surrounding farm lands and natural habitat. People have been arrested and convicted in many countries for starting fires which led to the loss of property and life. In most cases you will be making your fires in existing camp fires but caution should be exercised nonetheless
- Fires like to burn upwards and need plenty of oxygen
- To start a fire, build a little structure starting with a couple of medium sized logs on a dry surface. Lay the logs parallel to each other and place your fire starting material in the centre, see next paragraph. Place another couple of parallel logs at a right angle to the first two. Now pack twigs and thin, dry branches in the middle of the structure, taking care not to compress the fire starting material. Continue to build your structure adding more parallel logs, using larger logs as you build. You will eventually have what looks like an inverted wood pyramid. Be careful not to make the structure unstable. Light the fire starting material with a few matches, light below the thinnest material at the base and watch the fire grow while sipping on the refreshing beverage of your choice
- When lighting charcoal, you will need to follow a similar procedure allowing the fire starting material to burn from the centre outwards.

Here are a few suggestions for fire starting material and methods to ensure that they burn efficiently.
- Twisted newspaper. I was taught this method by a Swiss man with a red beard who had been taught by an Argentine with beer breath. Lay out a few sheets of newspaper. Fold the rectangular

sheet lengthwise in half then in half again. Working from the centre twist the paper in on itself until you reach each end and have a tightly twisted length. Have a large beer or wine bottle readily available. Tie the newspaper around the bottom of the bottle using a simple under and over knot. Repeat this procedure of twisting the newspaper and tying it to the bottle until you have five or six rows. Place the bottle in the centre of your fireplace and gently push the paper off the bottle. Place your logs around and above the little paper kraal, light a few pieces of newspaper and insert into the paper kraal and continue to build your fire structure. Drink the beer or wine

- My personal favourite fire starting method was taught to me by a very hard working Venezuelan, who had hand built an oasis in a town full of drunks and inflatable's. Shape either a handful of toilet paper or paper napkins into a bowl between the first two logs, as explained above. A few table spoons of cooking oil pooled in the middle will provide a fuel source which will burn for at least ten minutes. Light the edges of the paper and build the fire structure as above. Do not drink the cooking oil. If using this method with charcoal, follow the following procedure. Place the desired amount of charcoal in the centre of your fireplace, hollow out the centre and place the paper in the bowl shape in the middle. Add the oil and light the edges of the paper before carefully constructing a hollow coal pyramid around the flame being careful not to drop any coal into the oil pool and to not burn yourself. This takes a little practice but is highly rewarding and efficient. The only drawback of the paper cooking oil method is that your camp smells like a fish n chip shop, but this smell disappears within a few minutes, depending on the wind

- A small candle. You know those joke candles, the ones which keep reigniting once lit and blown out? These are perfect for making fires, particularly in windy areas, I am talking about you, Patagonia. In less windy areas, a small section of a normal table candle will do. Place the candle in the centre of your fire structure and light. Add twigs and small branches on top of, but not quite touching the candle. Continue to build your fire structure as described above. One thirty centimetre candle should be good for making six fires

- If you are shit out of luck you may need to use dry grass to get the fire going. Always remember that a fire burns from smallest to largest. Grass is not perfect because you need a lot to get a good consistent flame and the ashes can choke the fire

- Pine cones and dry coconut husks also make good kindling

- If the wood is less than perfect, you might have to encourage the flame by either blowing directly on the base of the fire or fanning the base with a plastic plate or a sturdy piece of cardboard.

Sometimes cooking over a fire will be the only option, perhaps your LPG has run out or you are having a problem with the cooker. Pots and pans with metal handles will fare better over open flames or coals than plastic or wood handles. Be careful though, those metal handles get hot. Cooking meat over a fire is an art form, there are those who do it very well and there are those who do it terribly. Generally those from the Southern Hemisphere do it best, as with most things outdoors, simply because of the favourable climate and our highly advanced brains. Just don't ask us to go outside when it is snowing. Here are some guidelines for cooking meat over a fire.

- Almost any meat can be made well over a fire

- Avoid open flames, which will burn the meat. Good strong coals are best. An easy way to know whether the coals are ready for cooking, hold your hand five centimetres above the grill for ten seconds. If it burns remove it. Your hand should be good and hot after nine seconds, if so you are ready to put the meat on

- Clean the grill with a wire brush and newspaper. Half an onion or lemon rubbed across a hot grill will remove most of the last Braai's grease and grime. Remember, you are cooking over high heat, the grill does not need to be shiny clean

- Have your tongs ready. The fire will usually have hot spots and you want to cook the meat evenly.

A water pistol is great to have on hand to shoot out the flames that ignite on the dripping fat. You can also shoot people with water if they take too long fetching your next cold beer.

CUTS OF MEAT

CHUCK - Paleta
Neck - Pescuezo
Shoulder - Paleta
Blade Roast - Diezmillo
Short rib - Costilla cargadas
BRISKET - Pecho
Stewing Beef - Res para guisar
SHANK - Brazuelo
Foreshank - Chambarete de mano
Rearshank - Chambarete de pata

RIB - Costillar
Rib roast - Costillar punta pequena
Short ribs - Costillar cortas
Rib Steak - Chuleton
SHORT LOIN - Lomo
Top loin steak - Bistek de lomo
T-Bone - T-Bone
Porterhouse - Chuleta de dos lomos
Tenderloin steaks - Bistec de filete
SIRLOIN - Aguayon
Sirloin steaks - Chuleta de aguayon
Sirloin tip roast - Aguayon en troso
PLATE - Agujas
FLANK - Falda

RUMP- Grupa
ROUND - Pierna
Top round - Bistek
Eye of round - Cuete
Tip roast/steak - Bola

The Braai

Roasting meat over a fire is a past time loved the world over. South Africans love it the most, seriously, and we call it a Braai (pronounced "brreye"). It could be below freezing but you will find the Saffa's outside, standing around a fire, a cold beer in one hand and a pair of tongs in the other. Ask any Londoner. A man will not let another man Braai in his home, in fact, if he even looks at the meat funny he will get a wedgy and a snot klap. But South African's, unfortunately, do not make the best Braai. That honour is reserved for the South Americans, specifically the Argentines, Uruguayans and the Brazilians and they call their Braai, Asado, or Churrasco in Brazil. They have wonderful cuts of meat, very different from Western cuts, with names like Picanha, Matambre, Bife de Chorizo, Entrana and Bife de Lomo to name but a few, which are specifically cut for cooking over a fire. Slow grilled, coated in coarse salt, the fat dripping through the meat, a glass of excellent red wine in your hand, a carnivore's culinary heaven. We had the honour of being taught how to grill by these fine men, maybe we will tell you how, but, because we are Saffas, we will call it a Braai.

First things first. Once you have mastered the art of making a fire you may find that fire, aka the Bush TV, not only provides enough heat and energy to cook a variety of meals but will also provide warmth and entertainment. There are few things more comforting than a good fire and a cold beverage, sitting down after a long busy day, thinking your thoughts.

Usually when you think of a Braai or a BBQ you think of those big, fatty slabs of meat, lamb chops and sausages and maybe an ignored salad. Or if you are from the USA you will consider a good BBQ to be either from the South or quick and easy Brats and Burgers made on the gas grill. I do love Brats and Burgers but that is most definitely not a Braai. When travelling long-term, you need to reassess the way you cook with fire and try and find ways to incorporate other food groups into the mix while saving resources and money.

One of the best, and most surprising Braais that we have ever eaten, was made for us by a happy bunch of vegetarian hippy Argentines in a beach camp in Northern Peru. The meal was sublime and so delicious I forgot about the lack of meat and the meal cost a fraction of what a meat Braai would have cost. They prepared a small fire and waited until the coals were just right, while sipping on red wine and strumming guitars. They then threw small potatoes, sweet potatoes and whole onions directly onto the coals, drank more wine, told some jokes, strummed the guitar and occasionally flipped the vegetables. Within 45 minutes the food was finished cooking, was removed from the coals, dusted off (not washed) and served with a fresh green salad, sliced tomatoes, olive oil and avocados, coarse salt and pepper. Delicious!

We make a similar meal on the fire in a tin foil package. Slice potato, sweet potato, eggplant and/or zucchini and onion and lay on a sheet of tin foil. Add olive oil, salt, pepper and garlic then wrap the tin foil over into a sealed package and place on the grill over a hot fire or directly onto coals. Olive oil prevents the food from burning.

Here are a few more grilled vegetable suggestions...
- Corn on the cob can be cooked from raw or par boiled and grilled or wrapped in tin foil with butter and placed on the grill
- Whole potatoes wrapped in tin foil, placed next to the coals as the fire is burning down to coals
- Red, green and yellow peppers, whole
- Sliced eggplant (zucchini)
- Carrots, whole.

Bread rolls can be heated on the grill just before the meal is served or, alternatively, you could make your own garlic bread out of whatever bread you have available, preferably a baguette or bread rolls.

- Slice and crush garlic and mix with butter, how much you use of either ingredient is up to you
- Using either the bread rolls or a baguette, slice and hinge open
- Lay the sliced bread on a sheet of foil
- Butter with the garlic and butter mix, close
- Wrap the foil around the bread twice and twist the ends
- Cook for five to ten minutes each side, depending on the heat of the fire. Be careful not to burn the bread.

To keep the beasts at bay, make a couple of starters.

- Remove the exposed centre stem from a few large mushrooms, place a few blobs of blue cheese in the "bowl" and grill face up on the grill until the cheese melts. Try to eat without messing
- Wrap whole peeled banana with rashers of bacon until the entire surface of the banana is wrapped. Use toothpicks to hold the bacon in place. Place on the grill and wait until the bacon is crispy, it takes a while, so be patient. Try and eat only one. Impossible
- Grill chicken wings which have been basted in olive oil. Fill a bowl of BBQ sauce and a bowl of hot sauce for dipping. Drool.

Grilled Chicken

The poor chicken. Why does it have to be so tasty? Everywhere you go people are boiling, grilling, deep frying or steaming this bird. It is served in fast food joints and Michelin star restaurant's; it is the food of the everyman. And it produces eggs. When man sets up his colony on Mars he will take two dogs and ten chickens along for the ride. Two of those chickens will be cocks. Only the French like to eat the cock.

Grilled chicken is delicious if cooked properly.

- To avoid burning the skin, a very common problem, marinade the whole chicken or pieces with olive oil, adding coarse salt and crushed pepper or hot sauce to taste
- A spatchcock chicken is a whole chicken cut in half along the backbone and hinged along the breast
- Be sure to cook the chicken throughout. Raw chicken may contain parasites which could make you very sick
- Cold, cooked chicken is great for salads and sandwiches so be sure to cook more chicken than you intend to eat in one serving

- Be creative with basting sauces, remembering to use olive oil as the base. It is best to baste the chicken with anything other than olive oil once it is almost finished cooking to prevent burning. You can either make or buy BBQ sauce, peri peri, or honey bastings. Use garlic sparingly, burnt garlic is bitter
- Drumsticks and thighs can be bought separately and are the most popular cuts for a Braai.

Red Meat

The Southern Hemisphere particularly has excellent red meat and industrialised farming is not as common down there where the sun shines warmest. Do you know why? Well, roughly 12% of the planets population lives in the Southern Hemisphere but we have 32% of the Earth's land mass. That's a lot of grazing. That is not to say there are no feed lots at all but far fewer than the United States and Europe. Generally, grass fed, free range animals are healthier, happier and taste better, with less guilty flavour. We try to buy meat in areas where animals range free and, if possible, avoid buying meat from chain stores. Meat is butchered differently in various parts of the world and you might need to do an internet search for the name of the cut you are looking for in that region. Write the name down and show it to the butcher. Often there are western style butcheries in large urban areas where you can get the cuts you are used to, but you may pay a premium.

Red meat is never cooked "well done" on the Braai. Never. Medium rare to rare with a well grilled outer is how good meat should be eaten. Often it is the sight of the red flesh and the blood which puts diners off rare meat but the reality is that meat with a good pink centre is by far the most flavourful and tender. Of all the cuts of meat our favourite is most likely the Picanha, or rump round. It is a large triangular cut about five centimetres thick with a one centimetre layer of fat. The fat really gives the meat an excellent flavour and should not be trimmed off. If you read a few articles on the different types of fat you will find that there is such a thing as healthy fat. This is the fat our Picanha wears to the party.

"Most people consider turkey, chicken, and fish healthy, yet think they should avoid red meat—or only choose very lean cuts—since they've always been told that it's high in saturated fat.

But there are two problems in that thinking. The first problem is that almost half of the fat in beef is a monounsaturated fat called oleic acid—the same heart-healthy fat that's found in olive oil. Second, most of the saturated fat in beef actually decreases your heart-disease risk—either by lowering LDL (bad) cholesterol, or by reducing your ratio of total cholesterol to HDL (good) cholesterol.
And besides being one of the most available sources of high-quality protein, beef also provides many important nutrients such as iron, zinc, and B vitamins. So the idea that beef is bad for you couldn't be further from the truth". Source, Men's Health.

It is on the Internet, so it must be true.

A good cut of meat does not need marinade or a bunch of fancy spices. Sprinkle the meat with coarse salt and a bit of black pepper and grill. Done. The trick is to achieve a balance of heat from the fire and grilling time. It is not always that easy, especially when you are often using different fuel sources and different size campfires and grills. Here is the process for a perfect Braai...

- Get the fire going with the best wood or coal available

- Crack a cold beer
- Tend the fire, being sure to burn all fuel evenly
- Now lay the grill over the fire to burn off any old grease and germ
- Put your tin foil vegetable packages on the grill and potatoes near the coals
- Replenish beer
- When the fuel has reduced to hot coals rub the grill with half a lemon or onion
- Float your hand 5 centimetres above the grill, feeling for hot spots
- Place the meat on the grill and enjoy the sizzle
- Using tongs, lift the meat periodically to check that is not burning
- Crush coarse salt over the meat
- Flip the meat when it takes on a golden grilled hue
- Replenish beer
- Have a sharp knife on hand to check whether the meat is cooked by making a small incision
- Steak should be pink inside, pork and chicken should not
- Gather the tribe
- Open a bottle of the good red
- Put a large wooden cutting board on the table and grind a little mound of salt in the corner
- Remove a few grilled pieces of meat and the vegetables from the fire, put the meat on the cutting board and open the vegetable packages on the table, using the tin foil as a bowl of sorts
- Cut bite sized slices of the meat
- The tribe pulls up a chair or stands by the fire and eats the vegetables and meat, dipping it in the salt and consuming hot, this is by far the most social and enjoyable way to eat Braai
- Remove more meat from the grill and cut on the cutting board. Try to get your hands on the fatty bits
- A tingle will start in your toes and make its way up to the top of your head. You have just had a food orgasm. You are welcome.

In some cultures, meat is cut very thin and then grilled. The reason for this thin cut is that the meat found in those regions tends to be tough and the best way to cook it is to either boil it in a stew or grill it in thin tasty slices. We want to avoid that meat.

Cooking with LPG

Cooking with LPG while travelling is just like cooking at home on your conventional stove. The one major difference is that you are cooking outdoors and have to contend with elements like rain and dust and the number one pain in the butt, wind. At times you will struggle to keep a good strong flame under the pot as gusts swirl around your rig. Before starting to cook, establish which way the wind is blowing and try and set up your cooking area using the rig as a wind break, a little effort before you start cooking will reduce cooking time and save precious fuel. Make sure that...

- All connections are kept clean and free of dust. A blocked connector will inhibit the flow of gas which will reduce flame strength
- If possible, buy a screw in stopper which will screw into the gas bottle outlet and prevent the ingress of dust and moisture in transit
- Keep all connections and hoses in a sealable bag
- Keep the cooker clean and check hose clamps regularly for leaks

- Ensure that you have the correct regulators and all necessary attachments and universal connectors
- Test your cooking system thoroughly before you leave home.

Food preparation

Herbs and spices are the building blocks of any delicious meal. Only the British cook without spices. Kidding Ma! Try to cook like a French woman mated with a South African man if you are a carnivore or you could just be a French woman. Breakfast, lunch and dinner recipes are interchangeable, it all depends on the time and ingredients you have available and what you feel like having for dinner. Bacon and eggs for dinner? Why the heck not? Eat whatever you want people, make your own rules.

The following spices and accoutrements should be knocking around in any good overlander spice box...

- Coarse sea salt
- Olive oil
- Coconut oil
- Paprika
- Black peppercorns
- Chicken, vegetable and beef stock (also great for making "instant" soups)
- Corn flour
- Cilantro
- Basil
- Rosemary
- Italian herbs
- Curry spice
- Star aniseed
- Cinnamon sticks
- Coriander seeds
- Chillies, dried
- Garlic
- Turmeric (incredibly healthy)
- Dill leaves
- Honey, substitute sugar with honey and watch the weight fall off
  Honey is amazing as it will never spoil
- Tomato paste
- Margarine is edible plastic, seek out good butter, salted or unsalted
- A small wooden pestle and mortar
- Garam Massala mix – you can purchase the herbs to make this mix on your own

The following herbs and spices can be used to compliment the following meats:

Thyme - Chicken, Pork, Beef, Lamb
Rosemary - Chicken, Pork, Beef, Lamb
Coriander - Chicken, Fish
Marjoram - Chicken, Fish

Sage - Chicken, Pork
Parsley - Chicken, Lamb
Chervil - Fish
Tarragon - Fish
Chives - Fish
Dill - Fish
Cilantro - Fish
Mint - Lamb

QUICK TIP: If you have a bulb of garlic and you're looking to peel the cloves quickly, pop them into a small container with a lid and shake it up. The friction removes the paper like skin and you're left with "clean cloves". You can then finely chop up the cloves and place it in a glass mason jar, filled with olive oil and pronto, you have a constant supply of garlic olive oil. Two birds with one stone

A challenge for many is to eat healthily, particularly when coming from a food culture where fat and sugar are ubiquitous. The good news is that you are almost guaranteed to lose weight and become fitter than you have been for many years while overlanding. The secret lies in daily activity, the glorious sense of fulfilment that long-term travelling provides and a change of diet. We have discovered that you can drink beer and wine almost daily, eat Braai every night and still lose weight. A lot of weight. The main weight gain culprit is a combination of processed foods and sugar. Especially sugar. It took ages for me to truly accept that drinking soda makes you fat. It was just something that my simple brain could not compute. Travelling the developing world, you will find that it is cheaper to drink healthy, pure juice from a fruit juice stand than it is to buy the equivalent amount of soda. You will find that you will have a healthier diet while travelling and it does not take a Herculean effort either. In many developed countries organic, natural food costs a premium, not so in the developing world. You will find fresh food markets in almost every town, farmers selling produce from the road side at an excellent price. Buy all your produce at one grocer and you will get a better price. In Ecuador we rented a house in the mountains while we completed our first book, We Will Be Free. The house was modern and fully equipped and we paid less than $15 a day. Every Sunday the man child and I would drive to the local market where we would stock up on the weeks' fruit and vegetables for less than $20. You can eat like a king and still be healthy. Natural fats in meat and sugars in fruit do not make you fat if you consume moderate portions. Hotdogs and soda and processed cheese make you fat, and miserable. By far my favourite treat is a fruit smoothie, if you don't have space in your rig for a blender, make space. There is a little blender called the Bullet and it is the perfect size to pack in your kitchen area. Being an overlander, you have plenty of time on your hands for food preparation, especially if you do not have children. Those little shits really do take a lot of time and energy, unless you are French, of course. You want some smoothie recipes?

Smoothies

There are a bunch of fanatics out there called juicers, they are best avoided, they all worship a skinny ex stock broker. Yes, he lost 150 kg's in twelve days, so what? Actually, juicing does sound pretty healthy. But, juicers are big and bulky and expensive. Ok, so you can get a small juicer for $50, that's a lot of beer money. Smoothies use the entire fruit with the exception of the peel and seeds. You can make combinations out of any fruit and pour it down your throat without the effort of chewing and spitting out seeds. A smoothie a day and you will be as regular as sunshine (the sun is always shining above the clouds) and glowing similarly. Blend whatever fruit is available and in season. Over ripe fruit is great in the blender, less waste. Smoothies are also an excellent replacement for other sweet treats such as chocolate. A moment on the lips, helps slim the hips. It's a pleasure. Send money..

Watermelon Smoothie

Watermelon is pretty much the healthiest thing you can put in your body. Only two things are healthier, water and coconut water. The best watermelons are medium sized, as are the best coconuts. Chop the watermelon into chunks and deposit in Ziploc bags. Allow to cool in the fridge overnight. If you have access to ice you can skip the cooling process. Let's assume that you have ice. Blend a third ice with two thirds watermelon, add honey if the watermelon is not sweet. Consume. There is only one thing better for a hangover. You guessed it, coconut water, so hydrating that you can use it as a substitute for a saline drip.

Other great smoothie combos are...
- Strawberry, mango and banana
- Mango and pawpaw
- Mango and honey melon
- Blackberry, raspberry and strawberry
- Peach, banana and mango
- All the above.

You can also make a variety of green smoothies or blend pumpkin and butternut as a thickener for curries and stews.

Breakfast

You wake up and roll out of bed, take a stroll to the nearest tree and return thirsty and famished. The first order of business is to get the kettle on the go, who can start the day without a cuppa tea or coffee? Unless you are in a long-term camp, you probably want a quick and easy meal. Whatever you usually eat for breakfast at home is what you should eat on the road unless you are into a daily fry up. Usually a bowl of cereal with milk or muesli and yoghurt and chunks of fruit is enough to get a normal person through to lunch. If you are like us and you love a slice of toast in the mornings, you may be having to make an extra effort. Lugging a toaster around is doable but often you will not have the electricity needed to run the energy eater. Making toast over a fire is also possible but most often making a fire in the morning is an unnecessary effort.

Here are a few breakfast recipes to help start the day like it bloody well should. If you are not in a rush to hit the road and need a good feed before a busy day. Quantities are based on a family of four. Halve for a couple or one teenager.

Toasted bacon and egg sarmie

This meal can be made either over an open fire or over the gas. It is a one frying pan meal; we are trying to keep dishes to a minimum.

Bacon	-	two rashes per person
Egg	-	one per person
Tomato	-	one large or two small
Onion	-	one medium, yellow, red or white, whatever you can get your hands on

Butter	-	salted, life is too short for unsalted. Margarine is disgusting
Sliced bread	-	two slices per person
Sliced cheese	-	one slice per sandwich, optional

Chop the rashes of bacon in half, slice the tomato 5mm between slices, do the same with an onion. Fry the bacon in a dry non-stick pan until the fat liquefies then pour out the fat and add the tomato and onion. Cook until the tomato starts to wrinkle and the onion starts to brown. Remove the mix from the heat and spoon onto a plate. Fry up the eggs, Sunnyside but not completely cooked, use a lid to help the eggs cook evenly. Put the optional slice of cheese on a slice of bread, add the bacon, tomato and onion, add coarse salt and ground pepper then add the egg, gently add the top slice of bread. Repeat the build process, a good sized pan should hold two sandwiches at a time. Spatula both sarmies into the pan, side by side and fry until the bread toasts, shake the pan gently, slip some butter into the pan and gently flip the sarmies with the spatula and a hand to hold it all together. If you are gentle enough you will not break the yolk of the egg.
Serve the yummy toasted awesomeness, let someone else do the dishes. The cook don't do dishes.

Eggs In A Basket

Another solution to the lack of a toaster is the ingeniously simple Eggs In A Basket. It is quick and easy to make and hits the spot every time. You will need:

Eggs	-	one or two per person
Sliced bread	-	one or two slices per person
Butter	-	a teaspoon

Lay the bread slices on a bread board and, using a cup as an improvised "cookie cutter", cut a circle out of each slice. Heat the frying pan to a low heat, add the butter and lay two slices of hollowed bread in the pan when the butter begins to bubble. Fry the bread and the cut out circles of bread in the butter until it is golden brown then flip. Crack an egg into the centre of each slice. Cover the pan with a lid until just before the eggs are cooked. Remove the lid, you want to release the moisture and let the bread crisp for a minute or two before serving with the toasted circles. . Season with coarse salt and crushed black pepper and Tabasco sauce if that's how you roll.

French Toast

Of course you know how to make French Toast but do you know the history of the crowd pleaser? "According to the Apicius, a collection of recipes from the early 5th century AD, the dish we now know as the French toast existed as early as the age of the Roman Empire. In their style of French toast, called Pan Dulcis, Romans would soak bread in milk (and sometimes also egg) mixture, then fry it in oil or butter". Old stale bread can be revived by soaking it in the egg. These days, store bought bread would rather turn green before it goes stale but an old school bakery bread, the good stuff, still tends to harden. We like to whisk the eggs with a bit of cream and a pinch of salt then fry in butter. The man child and I eat our French Toast with grated cheese while the girls tend to eat it with syrup or honey. When I was a kid I once ate nine slices in one sitting, those were the days. . . .

If you are in an area with plenty of tropical fruit you may want to try new ways to incorporate that healthy goodness into your diet. Fruit is natures greatest luxury and the health benefits are obvious. While waiting for dinner to cook, and you have cutting board and knife out, peel and chop any fruit you have, then put the resulting salad in a Ziploc bag and chill in the fridge. You can also serve some salad with whipped or fresh cream as dessert after dinner. In the morning the chilled fruit salad will be a healthy treat. You can add it to your muesli and yoghurt or you could eat it as is. Banana should only be added to the salad just before serving. Uneaten fruit salad can be blended into a smoothie.

Banana flapjacks

Banana flapjacks are quick and easy to make and delicious.

Ripe bananas	-	three medium
Self raising flour	-	one cup
Milk	-	one cup, maybe less
Honey	-	one table spoon
Salt	-	half a teaspoon.
Eggs	-	two, medium
Nuts & chunks of chocolate	-	optional

Moosh the bananas in a bowl until properly mooshed. Add the flour, honey and salt and mix while slowly adding the milk. Count to fifty while mixing. The consistency should be runny enough to pour off a spoon. Heat the non-stick pan to a medium heat and grease with butter. Once the butter begins to bubble, use a tablespoon to scoop and pour in the mix, one tablespoon equals one flapjack. You should be able to get four or five in a pan. Wait. Flip. Shake it, shake it. When bubbles appear in the tops of the flapjacks it is time to flip them with your plastic spatula. Wait. Shake it. Serve with peanut butter or sliced strawberries or just scoff them as is.

The Morning After The Braai Breakfast

When making a Braai always grill more than you intend to eat for dinner. The left over steak, chicken, sausage, pork and grilled vegetables can feed you for the next couple of days, a great treat when you are driving long distances and a peanut butter sarmie just won't do. The following breakfast fry up is the stuff dreams are made of.

Onion	-	1 medium
Tomato	-	2 medium
Egg	-	1 or 2 per person
Grilled meats	-	two handfuls of whatever you have
Tomato paste	-	2 table spoons
Braai sauce	-	2 table spoons (optional)
Butter or olive oil.		

Slice the tomato and onion in 5mm thick "rings" and fry in the butter or olive oil and add the tomato paste or Braai sauce. While the mix is browning, chop the meat into chunks or slices, depending on the meat, add to the pan. Once everything is sizzling nicely, scooch the meat, onion and tomato one side and crack a few eggs into the pan, cover with a lid until the eggs are almost done then remove the lid. Season with coarse sea salt, a sprinkle of paprika and pepper and serve on a buttered bun. Freaking awesome. You could also serve the meat, tomato and onion mix with Eggs In A Basket.

Lunch and dinner

As you are exploring the planet by vehicle you will be spending plenty of time either driving or as a passenger. Initially you may find yourself doing very long driving days but, eventually, you will find that a slower drive with more frequent stops is more rewarding. The Retired Couple knows this well and they will drive with the intention to enjoy the day as much as possible. They will stop for lunch under a tree or at a quiet area beside the road, they will take the time to eat salad and fruit and make a cup of tea. This is the best way to travel. Often, though, you will find yourself in a situation where you will have to drive long and hard to get to the ferry in time, through a built up megalopolis or through a dangerous area of a country where a civil war is being fought and the next safe "harbour" is relatively far away. Take ten minutes in the morning to pack a snack bag which should contain…

- Drinking water for all the crew
- A flask of coffee or tea
- Fruit, whatever is locally available
- Snack bread, high fibre if possible, topped with ham, salami, gouda or cheddar cheese. Your co-pilot can prepare these snacks when the road is not too bumpy or winding
- A bag of salted popcorn. Make your own popcorn in camp, a cheap, healthy snack loved by all
- Biltong for South Africans and jerky for Americans

The same snack bag will make a perfect daily picnic when you find a nice bit of lawn or a tree to relax under. Do not picnic in the middle of a civil war unless you are willing to share everything. When not travelling against the clock, take the time to slow down and watch the world go by. You are usually only in a rush if you over commit yourself.

The biscuit (or cookie as the Americans call it) is loved the world over for a very simple reason. It is usually delicious, easy to make using many of the ingredients needed to make bread and does not require cool storage. In Africa you will see people riding bicycles loaded high with biscuits and most stores will stock a good variety. In remote areas where chocolate is either unavailable or very expensive, the biscuit is your best option for a sweet snack.

By far the most enjoyable lunch for us is the gourmet sandwich, a combination of salad and bread and any meat, preferably topped with avocado, olive oil, coarse salt and ground pepper. Wash that down with a smoothie or fruit juice.

Other lunch options include the wrap, the taco, the tortilla and the simplest lunch of them all, pita bread and hummus. You have not lived until you have lunched with Palestinian construction workers, breaking pita bread and scooping spicy hummus out of a large tub. . . .

We often have quesadilla as a snack

1 bag of tortillas	-	2 tortillas per quesadilla
Grated cheese	-	to taste
Tomato puree	-	1 tablespoon per quesadilla
Sour cream	-	1 tablespoon per quesadilla
Avocado	-	mashed and salted, 1 tablespoon per quesadilla
Hot sauce	-	to taste.

Heat a frying pan to a low heat, do not grease. Lay a tortilla flat on the cutting board and spoon the tomato puree around the surface like you would a pizza base, sprinkle the cheese over the puree then lay another tortilla on top and place in the frying pan. You can busy yourself making more quesadilla's while waiting for the first quesadilla, which should be flipped with a spatula when golden brown. When both sides are done, slide it into a plate and put another in the pan. Garnish the cooked quesadilla with the sour cream and the avocado, sprinkle hot sauce, fold in half and feed. Voila, a vegetarian dish and you won't miss the meat. You can add tuna to the mix if you're looking for healthy alternatives.

Almuerzo (lunch) in Colombia is the main meal of the day for many and you can get a hot two course meal and fruit juice at almost any supermarket for about $2.
My point? For lunch eat what the locals eat, where the locals eat. You will usually find excellent value and will no doubt make a few friends. Or eat the local bread and be creative with the combinations of toppings. Peanut butter, preserves or Nutella on fresh bread was good enough when you were a kid and good enough during your midlife crisis.

No food should be wasted if you are going to be living on a budget, in fact it is a good idea to make double portions when cooking a full meal, that way you will have a ready cooked meal to heat and eat. There are always stray animals and human beings (think locals, Cyclists and Bikers) who could use a good feed. Stray dogs, if friendly, will thank you for a meal by becoming your guard dog or by running off with your shoes, you never know. In some places a temporary guard dog will deter dodgy humans and other animals from invading your camp. We had a little pregnant bitch adopt us in a camp in Ecuador, she knew we were carnivores and was guaranteed to have a few big bones to chew on daily. She took a distinct disliking to one particular biker and would chase him down the path, snapping at his heels if he came within ten meters of the Land Rover. I trusted that little dog, I did not trust that biker. Though we were tempted to take her along with us when we left, we knew that we would be adopting not only her but also her litter. We left her behind, sadly, but knew that she was in a good camp and that she was clever enough to get by. Also consider that taking on a new pet will cost a lot of money when it comes time to fly and ship to another continent. There will always be another stray waiting to be cared for, if only temporarily. If you are an animal lover be sure to carry a bag of dog food and a small water bowl for the poor critters you meet along the way. Be careful with strays though, particularly in Africa. If the locals treat the animals badly they tend to become more temperamental, less friendly and more opportunistic.
Back to food...

Arroz Carreteiro

This is a Brazilian dish from the southern Rio Grande Do Sul state, popular with the men and women who transported goods across the region with ox drawn wagons. Translated Arroz Carreteiro means Wagoners Rice. It is the perfect meal for a nomad, like yourself. Traditionally the dish is prepared using dried meat but we like to use our left over Braai meat. You can mix steak, sausage and chicken in the pan, it all tastes great. Similar to the Day After The Braai Breakfast, Arroz Carreteiro is a quick and easy meal, perfect for the end of a long, dusty, hung over day (when we Braai we always have a little too much fun). You will need...

-	Precooked meat	-	two handfuls, cubed
-	Onion	-	two medium, chopped
-	Peppers	-	green, red or yellow, chopped
-	Tomato	-	two medium, chopped
-	Olive oil	-	liberally splashed
-	Dried chilli	-	to taste
-	Garlic	-	two cloves, sliced fine and crushed
-	Turmeric	-	one tablespoon
-	Egg	-	optional, one per person

Boil the rice (slow boiled rice is better than speed boiled rice and makes less mess) and add the tablespoon of Turmeric to the water. In a pan, fry up the chopped onions, half the peppers and add a third of the tomatoes in a good splash of olive oil. Add the chilli and the garlic, allow to simmer. Add the chopped meat when the mix is nicely browned. Take a sip of beer. Lower the heat of the pan to low and add the rice to the mix, add coarse salt to taste. Just before the mix is ready to serve, add the other half of the peppers and the remainder of the chopped tomato. Splash more olive oil. Serve with fried eggs and a salad if you have the time, inclination and ingredients. Whatever is left over can be eaten with more fried eggs for breakfast or eaten, cold, for lunch. For a simple spicy rice dish, cook as above with bacon bits and sliced chicken breast instead of the leftover Braai meat.

Seafood

Next time you are in Mozambique head down to the coast and buy a bucket of massive prawns for the equivalent of $10 US. You could also buy a big crayfish or two depending on your hunger. For a few extra bucks you could have the prawn cleaned and de veined (or you could also eat the whole cooked prawn, head, tail, shell and guts like my good buddy Ria). Take the creepy crawlies back to your camp and chuck them on the grill while sucking on a big yellow bottle of Laurentina beer (be sure to clean the bottle or can with water and a wipe if drinking directly from the container). You will know that the prawns are ready to be eaten when the flesh turns from milky transparency to a firm pink. Have a frying pan with melted butter and garlic ready on the grill, put the cooked fokken prawns in the pan, pour in some Nandos hot peri peri sauce and squeeze a lemon over the prawns while they sizzle in the pan. Do the same with the crayfish tails. Serve with rice. Prawns are also known as shrimp or langoustines. Crayfish are very similar to lobster and are also known as crawdads, crawfish, fresh water lobster or mudbugs.

If you are a fisherman you will have a wonderful time catching (or trying to catch) your own dinner no matter where in the world you are. Or you can seek out fisheries and fishmongers when driving along coastal or freshwater fishing areas. Be sure to buy fish which does not smell too fishy, which has bright bulging eyes and red or pink gills. Once the fish is gutted and scaled, you can either fillet the fish or you can cook it whole. To cook the fish whole, you can spice it with coarse salt and pepper and cook it directly on a grill or you can add more flavour by cooking it wrapped in tin foil. Here is how...

- Chill a bottle of white wine
- Lay the clean whole fish on a large sheet of tin foil and cut from throat to tail (remove the guts if they have not already been removed)
- Stuff the fish with chopped tomato, onion and green/red pepper and marmalade in equal parts and add crushed garlic
- Sprinkle with olive oil, coarse salt and pepper (you may have noticed by now that we use these three condiments repetitively, remember, as overlanders space is limited and we must use what is readily available)
- Wrap the fish twice over in the foil, twist the ends and place over the coals
- Cooking time will depend on the thickness of the fish and the heat of the coals
- Serve when the flesh is white with a portion of rice and a salad
- Drizzle with lemon or lime
- Watch out for bones
- Drink the wine.

Lime and lemon are a fish's best friend, not only does the sour citrus add to the flavour of the meal but the acidity also "cooks" the fish. Ceviche, from Peru, is a wonderfully quick and easy dish made with fresh, uncooked fish and lime. Chop up the raw fish and place in a plate, add chopped tomato and red onions, throw in some leafy herbs, marinade the lot with a good dose of lime or lemon juice, pour on some olive oil, coarse salt and black pepper and eat. Scoop up the left over sauce with a piece of bread.

Jackfruit Pulled Pork Sandwiches by Ben Steiner

2 Servings 10 minutes Prep Time 20 minutes Cook Time

Ingredients:

For the pulled jackfruit:
2 cloves of garlic, minced
2 20 oz cans young green jackfruit in brine or water
2 tsp paprika powder
1 pinch red pepper flakes
1/4 cup vegetable broth
Black pepper, to taste

1 onion, chopped
1/2 tsp cumin
1/2 tsp liquid smoke
2 tsp brown sugar
3/4 cup BBQ-sauce
Salt, to taste

For the vegan ranch sauce:
1/2 cup vegan mayonnaise
1/2 tsp onion powder
Salt, to taste
1 tablespoon soy milk

1/2 tsp garlic powder
1 tbsp parsley, finely chopped
Black pepper, to taste

For the sandwiches:
2 buns
1 avocado
Servings Instructions:

1 tomato
lettuce

Drain and rinse the jackfruit. Remove the core and put in a mixing bowl. Stir in the spices (paprika, cumin, brown sugar) so the pieces are nicely covered.

In a medium pan, heat the olive oil over medium heat. Sauté the onion for about 3 minutes or until it becomes translucent. Then add the garlic and cook for another minute.

Add the jackfruit and cook for about 3 minutes. Then add the BBQ sauce, the liquid smoke (if using), and the vegetable broth and cook for another 15- 20 minutes. Use a fork to shred the jackfruit.

In then meantime make the vegan ranch sauce: Combine all ingredients in a small bowl.

Serve the pulled jackfruit on a bun together with tomatoes, lettuce, avocado, and ranch sauce.

Turtle Bars by Mark Maurer

Ingredients:
Graham crackers, enough to line 9x13 pan
1 cup salted butter
1 cup brown sugar
1 1/2 cup chopped nuts (pecans are my favorite!)

1 1/3 cup sugar
6 Tbsp milk
6 Tbsp salted butter
1/2 cup chocolate chips

Directions:
1. Line 9x13 pan with whole graham crackers
2. Slowly boil butter, brown sugar & chopped nuts for five minutes. Pour over graham crackers. Let cool
3. Boil sugar, milk & butter for one minute to make frosting. Take off heat & add chocolate chips. Beat until melted
4. Set pan in cold water & beat until right consistency to spread
5. Now spread chocolate mixture evenly over entire pan
6. Put in fridge to let everything set up firm. Cut into pieces and enjoy. Warning: these are very rich.....
too many and you are asking for a bellyache!

Buffalo Chicken Dip by Fernando Rivero

2 Chicken Breasts
1/2 cup Ranch or Blue Cheese dressing
2 sticks of Cream Cheese
Adobo

1 cup of Franks Red Hot Sauce
1 cup of Shredded Cheddar Cheese
Paprika

1. First season the chicken with Adobo and Paprika, throw the chicken in a pan and cook until it's fairly dry, about 15-20 mins
2. Shred the chicken with a fork and put it in any type of mixing bowl
3. Mix in the ranch dressing, franks sauce and cup of cheddar cheese
4. After it's nicely mixed, return everything to the pan on medium heat. When the mixture heats up, add the cream cheese. Let the cream cheese melt, mix it in thoroughly
5. Move to a serving dish and enjoy.

I like to use tostitos scoops but the dip can be eaten with pita, flat bread, crackers, etc...
Also this is not a spicy dish, if you want to add real spice I like to add about a 1/4 cup of Tobasco Habenero sauce

Very Simple by Tim Mann

Feeds 4

1 Package of Pita Bread
1 Can of Tomato Paste, or seasoned spaghetti sauce
1 Gouda Cheese (in the red wax)
1 Package of seasoned ground sausage or other meat of choice.
Butter/canola oil

In a frying pan or over open fire on tin foil, place the pita (bottom side greased w/ butter or oil)
Add thin layer of Tomato Paste or sauce

Add sliced or shredded Gouda Cheese
Add Meat (elk, buffalo, pig, etc)
Add more Gouda Cheese
Add salt or pepper as needed
Cover w/ foil & cook until cheese is melted.

When it's done, you have a hot, greasy personal backcountry pizza.

Beer bird

A favourite as it combines meat and beer in one meal. Get a whole chicken. Keep the innards for the stray dogs and cats. A quick sizzle on the fire should be fine for the gizzards. Grab a beer, preferably something pale (in a can of course), crack it, take a sip. You can add some garlic cloves to the can of beer and slide the beer inside the chicken. If possible, wire the legs together so the can is secured between its legs. Brush the bird with some olive oil and place on top of a grill, balance is key and difficult to achieve with a top heavy, upright bird. Some camping stores stock beer bird bases with a holder for the can and a wide base. You can either do this in an oven or over a fire. When done over a fire, it would be advisable to create a foil dome over the chicken and can in order to "smoke" it. Keep cooking it for a few hours and once the bird is done, do not consume the beer.

Luisa's Favourite Bread Recipes

Every nation has their own favourite type of bread. In the Middle East pita and unleavened bread, in the Americas, baguettes and dinner rolls, white loaf and tortillas, in East Africa they eat a flat bread called Injera and the Asians steam or deep fry their dough. Bread is the oldest known artificial food and is the cornerstone of diets the world over. There are those who refuse to eat bread (remember the Juicers, those who worship the skinny ex stock broker?) they are pale and unhappy. You have three bread choices whilst travelling, eat what the locals eat, seek out a good bakery or make your own. Or, if you are French, make a salad. Bread and potato eaters can eat salad all day long and never feel fed; I suppose it depends on your diet as a child or whether your mother is Irish.
If you choose to make your own bread you will need to practice either baking with a Dutch Oven over coals from a fire or you will need to invest in an oven. Coleman makes a little foldable oven which can be placed on a cooker top. Other flat breads can be fried or steamed.

Yeast starter
¾ cup of flour and 2 tablespoons
½ cup of water

Add the ingredients together and mix into a smooth batter. Place in a glass or plastic container and make sure that the sides are scraped down. Lightly place cling wrap on the top or place a lid ajar. It should have an even temperature of about 70F. Let sit for a day. Feed the starter with the same equal amounts as above. Repeat process for 4 days. By the 5th day, it should start bubbling/frothing and smelling pretty pungent or sour. If you're using it daily, then discard half of it and keep "feeding" it daily. If you only using it once a week, place in refrigerator and remove the day before using in order to yeast to recuperate. Once used, feed again and place in refrigerator the day after.

This is our best bread recipe, guaranteed, thanks to the Amish

1 cup water 110 °F
1 cup milk 110 °F
1/3 cup sugar/honey or maple syrup
1 ½ tbsp. dry yeast
1 ½ tsp salt
¼ cup coconut oil or vegetable oil
5 ½ cups flour

Heat the water and milk to 110 °F. Dissolve the sugar or pour in the honey or maple syrup. Measure in the yeast and whisk until dissolved. Let stand for 5 to 10 minutes until mixture is frothy. If it does not froth, use new yeast. Whisk in oil and salt and then add flour. Mixture must be sticky but not too wet. Knead for 10 minutes until silky and smooth. Lightly oil a bowl and let stand in a warm place for an hour or until doubled in size. Punch out the air and knead for another 3 minutes. Lard up two bread pans and divide the mixture evenly and roll into pans. Let rise for another 30 minutes and bake for 30 minutes at 350 °F

Some other "bread" options available:

Banana bread

3-4 ripe bananas
1 cup sugar
¼ tsp salt
1 tsp baking soda

¼ cup melted butter
1 ½ cups flour
1 egg beaten
1tsp essence

The problem with buying a bunch of bananas is that you usually eat a couple and the rest are ignored and in the heat of a vehicle begin to spoil. Making banana bread is a great use for those bananas which have blackened and lost the firm in their flesh. Mash the bananas and add the dry ingredients. Once well mixed, add the wet ingredients and mix well. Bake at 350 °F for 25 to 30 minutes

Pita bread

1 cup warm water
2 ½ cups flour
2 tsp olive oil

2 tsp yeast
2 tsp salt

Mix water and yeast and let rest for 5 minutes. Add 2 cups of flour, salt, oil and knead. Film the dough with olive oil and let it rest for 30 minutes. Divide in 8 pieces and flatten and let sit for 10 minutes. Use a rolling pin and flatten to 5cm in height and place on top of either a hot skillet and dry "fry" or on a baking sheet in the oven at 450C for 3 minutes until swollen.

Cornbread

1 can corn
½ cup sugar
2 large eggs
1 tbsp baking powder

1 ½ cups flour
½ cup milk
¼ soft margarine or lard
1 tsp salt

Mix all dry ingredients together and in a seperate bowl, mix all the wet ingredients together. Combine both mixtures and mix with a fork until smooth. Grease a baking tray of 30cm in diameter and bake for 25 minutes at 400 °F. Corn bread is a favourite Braai side dish. It is also a tasty as a road snack.

Hamburger rolls

2tbls yeast

½ cup vegetable oil

1 egg

3 to 3 ½ cups flour

1 cup and 2tbl warm water 110 °F

¼ cup sugar

1 tsp salt

Dissolve the yeast in water. Add the oil and sugar and mix well. Let it stand for 5 minutes. Add the egg, salt and some flour and mix. Knead for 5 minutes. Divide into 12 balls and flatten lightly. Place on a larded tray. Rest for 10 minutes. Proceed to bake at 425 °F for 8-10 minutes.

Dinner rolls

1 1/3 cup milk

¼ cup butter

1 tsp salt

½ tsp baking soda

2 eggs

4 cups flour

¾ tsp baking powder

2 ¼ tsp yeast

Blend yeast with 1 cup of flour, sugar and salt. Heat the milk and butte but go hotter than 130 °F. Add to the dry ingredients and mix. Beat eggs and add to the mixture. Add baking powder and soda and flour. Mix well and knead for 5 minutes. Rest until it has risen and divide into parts, slightly larger than a ping pong ball. Let rise for a bit and Bake at 350 °F for 12 -15 minutes.

RANDOM RECIPES

Chicken Lives Peri-Peri

This a perfect meal for breakfast, lunch or dinner. It can be prepared in bulk and kept refrigerated or frozen until you feel the need (perfect food for a hangover btw). You're going to need the following:

1 x 500g of organic or free range chicken livers

2 x red onions

1 x medium clove of garlic

1 x tbs of paprika

6 x tbs of olive oil

10 x cherry tomatoes

2 x peppers

1 x 250ml of tomato salsa or tomato puree

2 x cups of water

Chilli and salt to taste

- Chop the onions, garlic, red and green peppers
- Heat the olive oil in a large pot, add the onions, garlic and peppers - let them brown
- Add the cherry tomatoes and tomato puree, salt, chillies and paprika. Stir in the livers and leave to simmer for an hour to an hour and half
- Serve with a little white rice or fresh homemade bread

Chocolate cake

2 cups flour	1 cup sugar
¾ cup cocoa	1 ½ tsp baking soda
1 cup milk	2 eggs
1 cup boiling water	2 tsp baking powder
1 tsp salt	½ cup oil
2 tsp vanilla essence	

Blend wet and dry ingredients seperately. Once well mixed. Add the mixtures together and whisk for 2 minutes. Heat the water and add to the mixture - slowly!. Beat for 1 minute and place into two round 30cm in diameter larded/buttered pans. Bake in the oven for 30 to 35 minutes at 350 °F

Herbed cheese scones

2 cups flour	3 tsp baking powder
2 tsp dill	1 tsp salt
1/3 cup Lard or butter	½ cup cheese
¾ cup milk	

Mix the flour, dill, baking powder and salt. Cut in shortening with a blender or knife. Stir in the grated cheese and once crumbly, add the milk. Stir together to form a doughy batter. Roll out and cut out circles. Bake on a greased tray for 12-15 minutes at 425 °F.

Here are a few quick and easy meals that we prepare on a regular basis:

Pastas dishes are versatile and can be prepared quickly. We use a combination of minced meat, pesto or creamy bacon and mushroom for toppings
Lasagna - can be made meaty or vegetarian style

Cottage pie - perfect for those cold wintery nights, if you have an oven

Spicy rice - A quick and easy family favourite and you can either use chicken or minced meat

Stir-fry - Healthy and damn tasty

Fish - Perfect in many ways from cerviche, fish fillets to fish cakes

Chicken or meat pie - In South Africa we devour these at least once a week and can be accompanied with some mash and gravy, again, for those with an oven

Meatballs - Fill it with mozarella for the kids or have them in your pasta or even on a sandwich

Chicken a la King - a perfect dish for left over chicken after the braai

Curry - a Mutton curry is the best but chicken or even a vegetarian variation will do. Add some butternut for some texture and taste. Jessica likes hers with some sliced banana on the side

Prego rolls - Another quick dinner or lunch dish that can be prepared within 10 minutes. Thinly sliced meat does the trick and it won't cost a fortune

Hamburgers - Everybody loves a Burger - top it with some aged cheese or cream peppered mushroom sauce or just keep it simple

Mac & Cheese - It's a winner - bacon bits makes it even better

Pizza - the Classic crowd-pleaser - from vegans to meat eaters, this is a favourite for all family members

* accompany with a salad, if you have the ingredients available

	UNIT	METRIC U.S.		UNIT	METRIC U.S.
Capacity	1 ml	1/5 TSP	Butter	14.175 grm	1 tablespoon
	5 ml	1 TSP		4 ounces	1 stick
	15 ml	1 TBSP		1/2 cup	1 stick
	30 ml	1 fluid oz.		8 TBSP	1 stick
	50 ml	1/5 cup		113 grams	1 stick
	60 ml	1/4 cup		226 grams	1 cup
	80 ml	1/3 cup	Sugar	200 grams	1 cup caster sugar
	100 ml	3.4 fluid oz.		250 grams	1 cup raw sugar
	120 ml	1/2 cup		220 grams	1 cup brown sugar
	160 ml	2/3 cup		125 grams	1 cup conf sugar
	180 ml	3/4 cup		12.6 grams	1 TBSP caster sugar
	240 ml	1 cup	Honey	21.25 grams	1 tablespoon
	480 ml	1 pint/2 cups		340 grams	1 cup
	.95 liter	1 quart/4 cups	Yeast	3.1 grams	1 TSP i/dry yeast
	1 liter	34 fluid oz.		7 grams	2 1/4 TSP i/dry yeast
	1 liter	4.2 cups		9.3 grams	1 TBSP i/dry yeast
	1 liter	2.1 pints			
	1 liter	1.06 quarts	Cornstarch	150 grams	1 cup
	1 liter	.26 gallon		3.3 grams	1 teaspoon
	3.8 liters	4 quarts/1 gallon	Flour	125 grams	1 cup All-purpose flour
				120 grams	1 cup w/wheat flour
Weight	1 gram	.035 ounce	Cream	240 grams	1 cup
	14 grams	0.5 ounce		120 grams	1/2 cup
	28 grams	1 ounce		15 grams	1 tablespoon
	113 grams	1/4 pound (lb)			
	151 grams	1/3 pound (lb)			
	227 grams	1/2 pound (lb)	FAHRENHEIT	CELCIUS	
	454 grams	1 pound (lb)	250 ºF	120 ºC	
	500 grams	1.10 pounds (lbs)	275 ºF	135 ºC	
	1kg	35 oz/2.205 lbs	300 ºF	150 ºC	
			325 ºF	165 ºC	
Equivalents	1 cup	16 TBSP	350 ºF	175 ºC	
	3/4 cup	12 TBSP	375 ºF	190 ºC	
	2/3 cup	10 TBSP & 2 TSP	400 ºF	205 ºC	
	1/2 cup	8 TBSP	425 ºF	220 ºC	
	3/8 cup	6 TBSP	450 ºF	235 ºC	
	1/3 cup	5 TBSP & 1 TSP	475 ºF	245 ºC	
	1/4 cup	4 TBSP	500 ºF	260 ºC	
	1/6 cup	2 TBSP & 1 TSP			
	1/8 cup	2 TBSP			
	1/16 cup	1 TBSP			
	2 cups	1 pint			
	2 pints	1 quart			
	3 TSP	1 TBSP			
	48 TSP	1 cup			
	16 TBSP	1 cup			

Overland travel consists often of many days and even weeks of lonely travel, just you, your people and your rig. Out there, you will encounter two types of people, the hardy locals and the traveller. Meeting a fellow overlander in a remote part of the world will often be the beginning of a life long, long distance relationship. These people are your tribe, they are just like you even though they could probably not be more different. You share a passion and a determination. They are your new family.

The following overlanders travel according to their own rules and follow their own compass, we are proud to know them, we treasure them, they are alive! We asked each a series of questions, combined they have decades of experience, all answers are here in their words for your enlightenment.

Jan and Leone Vorster

Jan and Leone are a South African couple who have been travelling intermittently since the 1960's. They have been to 111 countries on six continents and have not reached an end.

Names:	Jan & Leone Vorster
Nationality:	South African
Make of vehicle:	Land Rover Forward Control Series 2B, modified
Period of ownership:	Since 1998
Self-built/commissioned/bought as is:	Self built (interior commissioned to my design)
4x4, 2x4 or other:	4x4
LHD or RHD:	Both (takes 2 hours to switch over)
Diesel, petrol or other:	Diesel
Mileage:	322 000 km from 1998 to 2015
Fuel consumption average:	18 litres/100 km
Camper, Roof Top Tent or other:	Camper
Make and size of tyres:	General 900-20
Recent breakdowns or major repairs:	Transfer case, Flywheel, Chassis cracks, Axle parts
Special vehicle specific tools carried:	Yes, some (Too specific to be of general interest)
Wish list for future modifications:	None
Dream Overland vehicle:	What we have
Favourite gear, gizmo or accessory:	Alternator that arc welds up to 185 Amps
Countries travelled overland:	111 countries on 6 continents
Website:	www.overlandhb.co.za
Best Memory:	Galapagos visit (and many others)

Summary of overland vehicle additions:

Electrical system
Solar Panels: 4x75W (Siemens)
Solar Regulator: 30A with charge & load protection (ProStar)
Split battery charging (from alternator)
Alternator: 12V/135A, 220V/2500W, welding 185A (Unipower)
Generator: 220V, 650W (Honda)   Battery charger from 220V: up to 20A continuous
Transformer 110V to 220V   Batteries: 3x105Ah deep cycle; 1x140Ah (for engine)
Inverter: 250W (ProWatt)   Lights, fans, water pump
Radio/cassette/cd player
Battery isolators: (Very heavy duty to handle starter motor current)
Freezer: 80 litre upright, 80mm wall thickness (Minus 40), 12V Compressor type
Fridge: 100 litre, front opening (Waeco Coolmatic CR110), 12V Compressor type
Note that brand names quoted are simply what I used and does not necessarily constitute endorsement of the product. There are alternative makes available.

Security
Camper rear door: upper and lower dead bolt locks, internal sliding bolt
Front doors: external original locks, internal sliding bolts + padlocks

Hinges on old Land Rovers: weld nuts to hinge pins, fit epoxy filled cap screws
Windows: Padlocked sand ladders or steel mesh screens, over all of them
Windscreen: Now 13mm thick (4 layers glass) laminated shatterproof glass
Previously padlocked steel mesh screen for shipping or longer parking
Padlocks: keyed alike, on all external items and screens. (We use up to 44)
Fire extinguishers: In cab and in rear
Security spray (Oleocapsicum): At all doors & above bed. (We may not have survived in Poland if it were not for this)

Self-recovery
Hi-lift jack: Fitted mounting & jacking points
Winch: Hydraulic (& kit)
Attachment points for up-righting when overturned (I needed them twice)
Axle diff locks, if side shafts can handle it (I had to remove them)
Compressor: tyre pump hose (Useful for sand driving)
Split wheel rims: To enable field repair of high (10,12,14) ply rated tyres
Lug/ road tread combination tyres: 2 spare wheels

Vehicle modifications
Very high air intake with ram & water release valve. (Height keeps dust out)
High capacity, two stage air filter (Donaldson)
Electric radiator fans: 3x two-stage units (AEG/Audi) (4 thermal switches)
Radiator mesh screen: removable Nylon
Oil cooler: (not mounted in front of radiator)
Fuel tanks: main 280 litres, reserve 65 l. (1500km range)
Fuel filter system: sedimenter/water trap, filter, second filter with water warn
Exhaust system: straight through, but well muffled, large diameter, stainless steel
Dual steering controls: takes 2 hours to switch between RHD and LHD
Power steering: ram type plus oil cooler for fluid which is also used in winch
Axle breather extension tubes
Springs: reinforced & modified for field blade change (bolted vs. forged clamps)
Heavy duty shock absorbers: gas filled
Mirrors: for all round view
Spot lights: front & rear
Head lamp stone guards
Roof hatch: No roof carrier, only alu flat strips for if tying on is needed
Propane gas cylinders: 2x18kg, externally mounted
Lifting slings & ratcheted tie-down straps: To lift vehicle into/out of container
Wind-out Awning

The Allie Family, Gary, Jo-Anne, Jade and Dane

The Allie family, from Port Elizabeth, South Africa set off for a round the world journey with family members in almost identical vehicles. Three years later the Allies returned to South Africa solo, after doing the world tour, having lost the other vehicles along the way. They had two young children who needed home schooling and Jo-Anne has told me, in confidence, that the most difficult part of the whole journey was getting the kids, especially the man-cub, to do their schooling. Her daughter has now entered medical school, determined to follow in the footsteps of her dad.

Nationality:	South African
Make of vehicle :	Toyota Landcruiser 4.2 Pickup
Period of ownership:	Since 2006
4x4, 2x4 or other :	4X4
LHD or RHD:	RHD
Diesel, petrol or other:	Diesel
Mileage:	210 000km
Fuel consumption average:	6km per litre
Camper, Roof Top Tent or other:	Camper
Make and size of tyres:	BF Goodridge 265/70 R16
Recent breakdowns or major repairs:	None
Modifications:	Campervan Conversion
Special vehicle specific tools:	None
Wish list for future modifications:	None
Dream Overland vehicle:	We have it!
Comments:	Very happy with Tipperdee!!!

Paul and Helen Crittenden. Going Overland

We met Paul and Helen in El Bolson, Argentina. They were heading South to Patagonia and we were heading North, escaping the encroaching winter. Their journey had already taken them from the UK to Russia (where they had collided with a horse in Siberia) and had braved Alaska in the middle of winter. We did some running repairs with the aid of the Land Rover Argentina club and settled down for a braai and an overlanding chat session. In Patagonia they had two more accidents, the first destroyed the new fender which they had finally replaced many moons after the Siberian horse dilemma, the second completely destroyed the Land Rover's rear axle. Paul spent the Patagonian winter working on the Land Rover in the outdoor parking lot of a hostel in Puerto Natales. To say the man is made of tough stuff is a bit of an understatement. From Argentina they shipped the newly repaired Land Rover to South Africa and drove back to the United Kingdom, arriving home after four and a half years of blood, sweat, tears and glory.

Nationality:	British
Make of vehicle:	Land Rover Defender 110 SW
Period of ownership:	2008 – 2014 (6 years)
Website:	www.goingoverland.com
4x4, 2x4 or other:	4x4
LHD or RHD:	RHD
Diesel, petrol or other:	Diesel
Mileage:	Chassis / Running gear 300,000km
	Engine and transmission 100,000km
Fuel consumption average:	9km/l
Camper, Roof Top Tent or other:	Roof top tent
Make and size of tyres:	BFG 265/75 R16
	(previously General Grabber AT2, same size)
Recent breakdowns/major repairs:	Breakdowns: None.
Repairs:	Fractured rear axle casing (fatigue)
	front diff crack (impact)

Vehicle Modifications

Rear side panel doors and internal storage, Brownchurch rack; ½ rollcage; winch; onboard water; 2x Aux tanks (+130 litres); ARB fridge; Dual battery; custom dash and airbox; Uprated suspension (std height).

Special vehicle specific tools:	Hub box spanner!
Wish list for future modifications:	Dustproofing; front and rear diff locks; upgraded transfer box diff peg; onboard air.
Dream Overland vehicle:	For really remote travel - the one I have

For a leisurely drive around the world – a Unimog with self designed box

John Brooks and Betti Doherty

John and Betti are the kind of people you wish you had always had in your life. Their positive disposition is infectious and a welcome relief from a world of pessimism and it is that attitude which serves them best despite the numerous challenges long term travelling has thrown at them. They have also been known to devote substantial time and effort to improving the lives of those they meet along the road. They inspire us. Burt, their Mercedes truck, was extensively modified with most of the design and fit being done by John and Betti and the result is fantastic. After three years touring the Americas they shipped Burt to Africa.

Names:	John & Betti
Nationality:	British, Hungarian
Make of vehicle:	Mercedes 1995, 1124
Period of ownership:	4 years
Website:	www.burtway.com
Self-built or commissioned or bought as is:	mostly self-built, then continuously rebuilt, it will never be finished
4x4, 2x4 or other:	4x4, diff lock
LHD or RHD:	RHD, never again!
Diesel, petrol or other:	Diesel (and whatever it is they sell in Bolivia)
Mileage:	90,000 in 3 years.
Fuel consumption average:	5km for 1 litre on a flat road with a tail wind
Camper, Roof Top Tent or other:	Camper - big heavy but comfortable box
Make and size of tyres:	Michelin XZY, 385, 65/22.5 – good stuff
Recent breakdowns or major repairs:	Highlights were breaking both chassis rails due to the idiot that built the cabin mount Mercedes is great, it keeps going
Modifications:	Its all custom build
Special vehicle specific tools carried:	Fairly big hammer
Wish list for future modifications:	Sell it and start again, truck travel is fabulous, just need to shed weight to get to those tucked away places
Dream Overland vehicle:	It depends where we intend to go, but definitely not anything built or designed by a British company - I prefer driving to fixing
Favourite gear, gizmo or accessory:	Proper front loading washing machine!

Comments

"For us travel is a gentle activity, to enjoy it we go slowly. Next time... If we can do this again I would do much the same. Listen to very few people's advice and go where it feels good to go. That is something we learned after a year or so on this trip and would again use more our feeling rather than intellect to guide us to the good stuff. As far as the truck is I would want a truck chassis again but make everything that goes on the chassis smaller, lighter and cleverer. It is very possible to have a good quality living space, good off road capacity and endurance yet make it lighter. The Mercedes commercial vehicle side of things is fabulous stuff. It is so overbuilt and strong, designed for hundreds of trouble free km's. I like living in the box, we never need to mind about seasons yet always have the option to live inside or out. So really, it is to do what we have done but a bit smarter.

Of course we all get good at the things we do if we do it for long enough. We, like you have got good at this, always room to improve but if we did this again we would be smarter, travel slower, skip passed the less interesting places and stay longer at the good spots. Sometimes we would have to leave a place to know how good it was, don't always realise at the time. But with experience we now know when we have found a good spot, this would help a lot for the next trip".

Gareth Griffiths and Lisa Grub

Names:	Gareth Griffiths & Lisa Grubb
Nationality:	British (or Welsh and English if you prefer)
Website:	www.siroccoverland.com
Make of vehicle:	Land Rover Defender 90 (300tdi)
Period of ownership:	2008 to present
Self built/commissioned/bought as is:	Self built
4x4, 2x4 or other:	Permanent 4x4
LHD or RHD:	RHD
Diesel, petrol or other:	Diesel, there is no other choice!
Mileage:	It is on 160,000 miles
Fuel consumption average:	10L/100km, 12-14L/100km towing
Camper, Roof Top Tent or other:	RTT
Make and size of tyres:	BFG MT KM2 (255/85r16)
Recent breakdowns or major repairs:	Nothing major. Had the exhaust shear off at the manifold, 2x UJ's, and an electrical short on our 2013 trip

Modifications

Extensive: roll cage, diff guards, HD sills, bullbar, winch (upgraded), HID driving lights, 50mm OME EHD suspension, Wide angle front propshaft, LSD front and rear, stainless exhaust, wheel carrier, shelf system in rear, rear window guards, rear door table, upgraded seats, cubby box, upgraded dash, RedARC dual battery system, solar, battery monitors, Oil pressure/temperature gauges, several 12v outlets, heated mirrors, heated windscreen, work lights, Hannibal rear awning, maxtrax mounted to roll cage, TD5 60L rear fuel tank transferred by 12v pump (separate gauge), Engel fridge on slide, 150w Pure Sine inverter, cargo barrier, ARB compressor hard mounted, Anderson plugs front and rear, 14" steering wheel

Special vehicle specific tools carried:	None, keep it simple!
Wish list for future modifications:	Front Runner gull wing sides to improve storage and access
Dream Overland vehicle:	MAN CAT!
Favourite gear, gizmo or accessory:	I love the comfort of my Kermit Chair and my Engel Fridge. Our trailer is also a pretty cool build. I have been rebuilding it for the MKII version for our next adventure. It is all ready much better than it was when we left the UK!
Countries travelled overland:	Europe, The Balkans, Australia, The Stans, North Africa, East Asia
Best Memory:	Too many great times on the road to list 1... or even 5

Knowing what you know now, if you could do one thing differently, what would you change? I don't think I would do anything differently to how we have done it. We haven't found any major pitfalls with our methods of travel etc. Sure it would be nice to have a big Unimog but I wouldn't have done all the travelling I have done as I would still be saving up for one! Our little 90 also gets to far out places bigger vehicles just physically cannot go.

My parting advice for those starting fresh would be:
I wouldn't listen to everything everyone says online. It is the greatest source of info but on the other hand people over complicate every single facet of overland travel and if you are just starting out it can become daunting and overwhelming. Sift through the crap spouted by so called 'experts' and 'veterans' and don't trust the magazines or those with hidden agendas.

Start basic, go camping, work things out logically for yourself and take everything everyone says with a pinch of salt. The main thing is just to get up and go. Don't let fear, self doubt, the naysayers, or lack of equipment stop you. If you want to go, just go, everything will be alright in the end.

Lizzybus David and Jane

These guys are simply nuts. I know this for a fact even though we have never met them. Being a long term traveller you are part of a tribe, a tribe spread across the four corners of the globe. We are connected through each other essentially, it is not uncommon to meet someone in Africa who has been hanging out with someone in Asia at some stage and then you meet the someone from Asia in Alaska and you have a beer and chat warmly about the mutual friend who is currently, probably, off grid in their rig somewhere very far away. When you connect with an old traveller friend months later the first question is invariably, "So, where are you now". "Agh, I am in India mate, doing a stint with a telecoms firm then I will be heading back to the truck in Mongolia". It is all just too bloody charming. And though the Lizzybus camp and ours have never, it is merely a matter of time before our paths cross, meat shall be burned and cold beverages consumed.

This is their story in their own words...

"On 16th August 2009 we came up with what we thought was a brilliant idea, to buy one of those Land Rover things and drive it around the world. So we quit our jobs, sold, donated and trashed our possessions', rented our houses out and set off on a wing and a prayer in a Land Rover we named Lizzybus. David a Legal bod, I worked in IT not exactly the best qualifications for what lay ahead, more like lambs to the slaughter.

Our friends and family reckoned we'd make it to Dover maybe even France, we just headed South via the West Coast of Africa. Six months in we hated it, the pollution, poverty, corruption, having lost over 4 stone between us, washing in buckets living in a box. But then it all changed, we no longer compared, we embraced, we no longer cared we shared in the lifes or people around us, saw only the distant horizon and what adventures lay ahead, we were HOME.
For us both, it has been the most humbling amazing experience, to anyone ever thinking about travel in any way, a week a month a year anything, leave all your pre-conceived ideas at home, never judge, just observe and most important of all Just Do It!"

Names:	David Turner (55) – Jayne Wilkinson (58)
Nationality:	English
Website:	www.lizzybus.com
Make of vehicle:	Land Rover Defender 1998
Period of ownership:	8 Years
Self built or commissioned or bought as is:	Self Built
4x4, 2x4 or other:	4 x 4
LHD or RHD:	RHD
Diesel, petrol or other:	Diesel
Mileage:	250,000 mls
Fuel consumption average:	28 mpig
Camper, Roof Top Tent or other:	Roof Top Tent (5 Years) converted to Pop top
Make and size of tyres:	BF Goodrich 235/85 R16 MT
Countries travelled overland:	6 Continents – 66 Countries – 136,000 miles – 6 Years .... so far!

Recent breakdowns or major repairs

We have had what you would expect of a vehicle driven off road for six years:

Clutch x2	Brake Callipers replaced	UJ x2
Panhard bushes	Prop Shaft x2	Wheel bearings x2
Drive shaft	Water pump	Brake servo
Clutch master cylinder	Gearbox	

Lizzybus has undergone a complete re-build internal & external ready for her next trip

Modifications

Just basic overland stuff:

Long Range Tank

Water Filter System

Second battery system (now changed from split charge to double alternator)

Heavy duty suspension

Uprated rear drive shafts

Special vehicle specific tools carried:

David would say a basic tool kit, I would say an extensive tool kit!!!!! Plus Imperial spanners/sockets. Water pump spanner
Hub nut socket

Wish list for future modifications

After our five year trip we have just re-built Lizzybus, this was our wish list/priority

Our focus for the re-build was: Security. Internal access to get from your sleeping "quarters" to be able to drive away, (we had the classic roof tent & in the Congo three very big guys with knives tried to rob us) If in danger you need to flee not fight

Weight: Keeping the vehicle as light as possible

Stealth: We wanted a conversion that allowed us to sleep inside when in cities or in insecure areas or when gale force winds made opening a roof tent impossible.

Favourite gear, gizmo or accessory: Sid a black mamba plastic snake for intimidating the masses

Ikea wooden shower tray placed at the foot of the ladder with a bucket of water serves to rid feet of any putrid smells and washes off debris/sand before getting into the tent.

Best Memory

Arriving back to the UK on 21st November 2015 having by some miracle managed to get ourselfs and an old Land Rover around the world and realising we had not murdered each other, were still talking and more importantly wanted to carry on traveling!!!

Comments

"ONE LIFE LIVE IT!!"

Lizzybus David and Jane in Spain

Georg & Andrea at Cape Agulhas

Georg and Andrea

Georg and Andrea Schonberger are a German couple who toured the Americas and Africa extensively in their Land Cruiser. Georg absolutely adores the Land Rover Defender but would rather swallow his own tongue than ever admit this guilty little secret. They visited us in South Africa in the months before we left for South America and were able to give us some great tips and insight into the Pan Am experience.

Make of vehicle:	Toyota Landcruiser HZJ78, 2001, DesertTec conversion
Period of ownership:	Bought in 2007, then rebuilt and made "trip worthy" - still in my possession, you will have to cut out the steering wheel of my cold hands...
4x4, 2x4 or other:	4x4
LHD or RHD:	LHD
Diesel, petrol or other:	Diesel
Mileage:	159.000km (127.000 on the trip)
Fuel consumption average:	13.2 L / 100km - avarage of the whole trip
Camper, Roof Top Tent or other:	"other" - we have a camper like hardtop to sleep in
Make and size of tyres:	BFG 285/75 R16 one(!) puncture in 127.000km! (but I would rather go for 255/85 R16 the next time)
Recent breakdowns/repairs:	None, I maintain it to death...

Modifications
Long range fuel tank (250L + 90 original), water tank (100L), solar power/charger (120W), winch (WARN), OME 3 inch lift + complete heavy duty suspension kit, a complete kitchen with Engel fridge / bedroom – oh, and don't forget this "girls only pipi box" of course

Special vehicle specific tools
Big hammer and a screwdriver; come on, its a Toyota I only needed my tools to fix Land Rovers along the road - serious: 55mm nut to adjust wheel bearings

Wish list for future modifications
None. Ok, if I would have the money I would fit the engine, gearbox and axles of the Toyota HD80 as well as 9.00R16 truck tires. Which would involve cutting out the fenders and refactoring the whole steering geometry as well. But they look just awesome...

Dream Overland vehicle
Steyr 12M18 with a converted army radio container/shelter and 14.00R20 truck tires

Comments
Where can I get this beer now?

Michel & Ursi Buchs – Paws on Tour

Michel and Ursi Buchs shipped their 1993 Land Cruiser HZJ75 to Alsaka in 2012 and then set off for South America where their journey ended in 2015. They are truly courageous explorers who actively sought the road less travelled while taking care of the Cruiser and two old dogs, Miro and Sheelah. Their photography is simply sublime. We would highly recommend that any off-road loving overlander traversing the Pan Am should take a look at the GPS waypoints on their website, under the heading Downloads. They found the toughest, most beautiful routes and have diligently kept records of not only their route but also of other travellers.

Nationality:	Swiss-Colombian & Swiss
Website:	www.pawsontour.com
Make of vehicle:	1993 Toyota Land Cruiser HZJ75
Period of ownership:	2010-2016
Self built or commissioned or bought as is:	70% bought as is (frame off resto) and 30% self built (about 400 hours self built)
4x4, 2x4 or other:	4x4
LHD or RHD:	LHD
Diesel, petrol or other:	Diesel
Mileage:	298'000km on clock, +- 127'000km on this trip
Fuel consumption average:	avg. of 13-16liter/100km or 18mpg- 14.7mpg In Sand even more!
Camper, Roof Top Tent or other:	Camper cabin, European style
Make and size of tyres:	Toyo MT & now Goodyear MTR Kevlar 285785R16

Recent breakdowns or major repairs
Ecuador transmission counter shaft main bearing failed, 5 days in Quito fixing the trans: http://www.pawsontour.com/iea/berichte/Ecuador/Woche-29-bis-30/woche-29-bis-30.html

Modifications
LOTS... OME suspension, Turbo with boost compensator, AC, HD Cooler, Lithium Batteries all the way, Separ Diesel Filter, 24/12VDC converter, 230W Solarcell with MPPT, 10liter hot water boiler, Seagull Filter System with 100liter water tanks, VIAR400 on frame, 50l Waeco fridge, 11kg aluminium gas bottle, flood lights all around, Espar 5kW water heater with altitude kit, floor isolated in front, EBC brake pads with slotted/drilled discs, 285 tires with 16x8 rims, special front bumper with water & tool compartment, 12'500lbs winch, 4 sand ladders etc. etc. etc.
Special vehicle specific tools carried – front wheel bearing 54mm socket, special 3 finger socket for rear wheel bearing, injection pump adjustment tool with gauge, feeler gauge for valve clearance check

Wish list for future modifications:	1HD-T engine with intercooler
Dream Overland vehicle:	Bucher Duro 6x6 and Dodge Power Wagon
Countries travelled overland:	North, Central and South America
Best Memory:	USA West, Mexico, Guatemala, Colombia,

Bolivia & Argentina
Comments – awesome trip! Will surely continue overlanding, but not that long anymore... 3.5years with almost everyday driving were pretty exhausting

Drive Nacho Drive

Names:	Brad and Sheena Van Orden
Nationality:	We hail from the USA
Website:	www.drivenachodrive.com
Make of vehicle:	Nacho is a 1984 Volkswagen Vanagon. It originally came as a full Westfalia camper, but we gutted it and rebuilt it as a marvel of overland hodge-podgery
Period of ownership:	We bought it in 2008 from a girl in Hollywood who lived with a puppeteer
Self built or commissioned or bought as is:	We built Nacho into his present likeness in the summer winds and winter snows of Flagstaff, Arizona
4x4, 2x4 or other:	2x4. Turns out that's all you need
LHD or RHD:	On the left
Diesel, petrol or other:	Petrol
Mileage:	When we set out on the road, Nacho had 276,000 miles. By the time we pulled back into the driveway that number had risen to around 322,000
Fuel consumption average:	With the 1.9L VW wasserboxer engine that we started the trip with, we got around 16 mpg or so. When we got to Thailand we replaced it with a 2.5L Subaru engine and it jumped to around 18.5 mpg
Camper, Roof Top Tent or other:	It's sort of a combo of both. The van's interior looks a lot like a miniature Japanese apartment, and the top pops up from the inside, giving access to the upstairs bed
Make and size of tyres:	We began with General Grabber AT2, 225 x R14 and replaced them with some Thai 225s BFGoodrich tires. They claim 195 x R14

Recent breakdowns or major repairs
It's always something. Transmission failure, failed brake master cylinder, starter, alternator, ball joints, tie rod ends, control arm bushings, and lots of wheel bearings

Modifications
Everything. We gutted the van and started over. It has a new engine and all new interior.
Special vehicle specific tools carried:
Nothing vehicle-specific, just a toolbar full of the usual tools.

Wish list for future modifications:
I've pretty much done everything I wanted to do on the grand scale. I wouldn't mind a new

exhaust system and some new urethane upper control arm bushings.
Dream Overland vehicle: We already own it!

Favourite gear, gizmo or accessory:
I would say we were most pleased with the solar electric system, our refrigerator, and the hot water system I built

Countries travelled overland
North, Central and South America, Asia, India, Europe

Best Memory
One that I think about a lot was when we were in Nepal. The Maoists declared a country-wide strike over a ten day period in which nobody was to open their business or drive on the country's roads, to disrupt the elections, which the Maoists opposed. We had intended to drive from Kathmandu deep into the Himalayas to begin the Langtang Valley trek. After consulting some police officers, we ended up writing "tourist" on our windshield with a bar of soap so as to avoid the Maoists' petrol bombs, and took off into the mountains and had the privilege of being the only vehicle on the road in all of Kathmandu, and were eventually absorbed into a military convoy into the mountains.

Comments
Becoming overlanders has been extremely fulfilling for us. We've learned so much about ourselves, the people who inhabit this world, and the places they live; this education can't be bought, it has to be lived.   Check out Drive Nacho Drive's two books at www.drivenachodrive.com.

Andrew Lord

Andrew is the quintessential long term Overland Biker

Name:	Andrew Lord
Nationality:	British
Make of vehicle:	BMW F650 GS Dakar
Period of ownership:	8 years
Self built/commissioned/bought as is:	Standard bike bought used. Customised for adventure riding
4x4, 2x4 or other:	Motorcycle
LHD or RHD:	Both
Diesel, petrol or other:	Petrol

Mileage – 195,000+
Fuel consumption average – 62 MPG
Camper, Roof Top Tent or other – Self standing tent
Make and size of tyres – Metzler Tourance and Continental TKC 80
Recent breakdowns or major repairs – Water pump

Modifications

Touratech hand guards
Custom light bar for LED lighting
Galfer stainless brake lines
Touratech chain guard
Jesse Odyssey side cases
Wolfman tank bag
Wunderlich LED rear light

Independent dimming of both lights
Galfer wave brake rotors front and rear
Touratech front mudguard
Mr Eds Moto custom fit ergonomic seat
Overland Solutions rear rack
Wolfman rack bag
All Balls Racing bearings throughout

Clearwater LED lighting with one off custom loom, 7 flash patterns
RAM mounts for Garmin GPS and Drift action camera
Featherlight clutch and throttle cables (spare of each pre routed ready to connect)
Wunderlich windshield customised for height
TFX shock – custom built with super duty preload adjuster and remote gas reservoir
Race Tech forks – Gold Valve Emulators, progressive springs
Overland Solutions heavy-duty side stand and foot pegs and foot peg hangers
High output charging system
Grease points added to headstock and rear suspension bearing housings
Swing arm end caps drilled and lock wired – F650s loose these for a pastime
Flexi oil return line – allows easier removal/replacement of engine side case for water pump maintenance
Additional fuel filter – pre-filters BMWs combined fuel filter/pressure regulator
K and N air filter
Scottoiler chain oiler
Burns Moto accessory fuse board
Heated clothing harness and controller
Custom built radiator shield
Burns Moto USB charging outlets front and rear

Burns Moto fused accessory leads – GPS, tire inflator etc.

Extensive spares kit including brakes pads, control cables, fuel and oil filters, cam chain tensioner, spark plugs, drive chain and sprockets, wheel bearings, 2 water pumps

Special vehicle specific tools carried
Customised socket for oil drain plug, spark plug wrench with flexi drive. C spanner for rear suspension

Wish list for future modifications
Simon Pavey custom side engine side case. – allows change of water pump without need to drain engine oil

Dream Overland vehicle
Honda CR250L specced by Andrew Lord with Burns Moto electrics, TFX Suspension, Andrew Lord designed luggage and custom gel seat

Favourite gear, gizmo or accessory
Nolan 140 flip front helmet and Exped deluxe air mattress

Countries travelled overland –
Europe, The Stans, Asia, Israel, Saudi Arabia, North, Central and South America

Imraan Sayed, Ria Moothilal and Jiten Magan

Standing under the blazing Malawian sun, six hours into a twelve hour wait for diesel, a lone long distance cyclist stopped a short distance away from the Landy. A South African flag hung from a fishing rod protruding from the rear saddle bags and the rider stood sweating, consulting a map. We had driven past him and his two friends on a mountain pass, waving and shouting encouragement as they laboured. I approached the bearded man and asked if he needed anything. He was tired and lost, separated from his two companions. He was not in the mood for a chat. I returned to the Defender and retrieved an Orange Maid ice lolly from the Engel freezer and offered it to the man, his name was Imraan. Imraan smiled broadly and for two minutes ate the large lolly with fellatial passion. I gave him his space and returned to chat once the stick was done being nibbled. He had a rendezvous with his friends at the home of a family friend. I told him that if he ever made it down to Cape Maclear on the banks of Lake Malawi, he should stay at Fat Monkeys. I wished him luck and he lumbered off down the road. A week later, Luisa and I were sitting at a table outside the Fat Monkeys pub. A cyclist, Ria, entered the compound through the large metal gates, joined us at the table and was greeted by a large, cold beer. A few minutes later a second cyclist, Jiten, joined us and was presented a cold beer and minutes later Imraan rolled through the gate and recognized me as the ice lolly man from Blantyre. By the end of the evening the entire table was covered with beer and Lupini Gold bottles. We sang songs and mocked everything Holy, a beautiful friendship was christened by liquid gold.

"The Boys" took nine months to complete the 11,500 kilometre journey from Cape Town to Cairo before returning to South Africa and travelling to our home for a reunion party. They also managed to raise a substantial amount of money for the Hear Us organisation which provides less fortunate people with life changing cochlear hearing implants. Legends. Check it out at www.siyashova.com

Nationality: South African

Make of bicycle: Custom built steel frame from a local frame builder. Built to provide quite an upright stance while sitting (less strain on back and wrists/get to take in more of the beautiful scenery) We chose steel so if we had any frame damage it could be welded to repair and apparently steel bends/flexes better under tension while loaded. Waterproof Ortlieb panniers (2 front/2 back/1 handlebar and 1 duffle bag behind seat). Tubus racks. Basic 8 speed drive chain and cantilever brakes for easier availability of spares in Africa. A must have brooks saddle. Chris King headset.

Period of ownership: With multiple delays/hiccups during frame building the bicycle was only ready 3 weeks before anticipated departure for Cape to Cairo cycle. Needless to say not much practice/training was done on the bicycle. 5 years down the line I still own this very special bicycle

Mileage completed on journey: around 11,500km

Special tools carried: Basic tool kit with Allen keys, puncture repair kit, spare brake and gear cables (only used 1 between 3 bicycles), spare tubes, spare foldable Tyre (not used), extra spokes (not used). Shifting spanner to tighten headset (not needed) spare brake shoes (not used) spare chain (was used and should have been replaced much earlier to prevent damage to cassette)

Dream overland vehicle: After having done a cycle journey I hope to do the next one an any vehicle with an internal combustion engine

Favorite gear/gizmo or accessory: My ipod while cycling. A stick with a V shaped fork at the end (picked up on route) used as a bicycle stand

Countries Travelled: South Africa - Lesotho - Swaziland - Mozambique - Malawi - Tanzania (including Zanzibar) - Kenya - Ethiopia - Sudan - Egypt

Best memory: Cycling short distances along the Western side of lake Malawi and staying at the multiple backpackers, just chilling and contemplating life. Cycling down the Blue Nile Gorge was also quite a memorable experience!

Top tips for future long distance cyclists: Pack light and downscale in your first few weeks If there are people there will be food and water. Interact with locals, you will be amazed at their generosity. Cycle shorter distances and take in the natural beauty, its not a race!

Knowing what you know now, if you could do one thing differently, what would you change? Cycling into a predominant headwind (Sudan) can destroy your spirit while being able to cycle downwind with minimal effort is such a joy. Don't only plan routes around rainfall patterns, also take into account predominant wind directions.

Joop and Adrie

Joop and Adrie are the Dutchest Dutch people you will ever meet. They wear clogs daily, have the hallmark Dutch sense of humour and have no idea what a braai is. Their DAF truck has a built in washing machine and hauls a motorbike, kayaks and Joop's paragliding gear. To be fair they once toured Southern Africa in a Suzuki Vitara so they have paid their dues. If you are searching for them look no further than the nearest windy cliff. Joop is a hands on kind of guy and he is not afraid to take the entire truck apart if there is a repair which needs to be done.

Make of vehicle:	DAF
Period of ownership:	4 years
Website:	http://joopenadriewaarheen.blogspot.com
4x4, 2x4 or other:	4x4
LHD or RHD:	LHD
Diesel, petrol or other:	Diesel
Mileage:	340 000 km's
Fuel consumption average:	25/30 L 100 km
Camper, Roof Top Tent or other:	Expedition truck
Make and size of tyres:	Goodyear 395-85-R20
Recent breakdowns or major repairs:	Lifting Cabin (Joop is being modest, this was a huge job)

Modifications
Double shocks (Again, Joop is being modest)

Special vehicle specific tools:	Leatherman and Air Jacks 60 ton.
Wish list for future modifications:	Batteries 4x220 amh
Dream Overland vehicle:	None, certainly not a Defender

YOU KNOW YOU'RE AN OVERLANDER WHEN.......

- You have no clue which day of the week it is or even the date
- You wear the same pair of shorts five days in a row
- Customs officials ask to take photos of you
- Young girls in remote little towns ask you if you have met Justin Bieber
- You know every single SUV, truck or bike tyre on the market, including its load rating
- Indoor plumbing is the ultimate luxury
- You can make a fire out of almost anything
- Cars pull up next to you on the freeway just to take a look and give you a thumbs up
- Random people congratulate you for just being you
- Shaving is optional and your feet are always dirty
- You repair everything you own to make it last forever
- Running out of duct tape is like running out of pasta
- A luxury campsite is defined as having reliable wifi, electricity and maybe a toilet seat
- For Christmas you give and receive car parts and tools
- Your shoes may be falling apart but you budget a bit extra for the really good tyres
- You spend so much time being lost, that you forget what the word lost really means
- You have friends from any nation around the world you've actually met and miss
- Your daily conversation revolves around which route to take, visa requirements, the budget and food
- You spend two hours a day looking for a campsite
- You find a good campsite and can't seem to leave
- You spend so much time covered in mozzie repellent you suffer from temporary amnesia and uncontrollable muscle ticks
- You forget what it's like to live in the "real" world
- Major news events go completely unnoticed
- The police and military pull you over just to take a look at you and your rig and ask, "were yol fromh"
- Your diet consists of food you have never tasted before, water, fruit juice, beer, pasta and bbq's
- Reading about the most dangerous places in the world, you realize you've been to or going to most of them
- Camping at a gas station, parking lot, in the middle of nowhere is totally normal
- You're always either boiling hot or freezing cold
- You start looking like a Rastafarian and not by choice
- Your first language starts sounding like your second language
- You finally see yourself in a mirror after being off the grid for so long that you're totally shocked at what you see
- Entering a chain supermarket you get excited to see bright lights and shiny things
- Doing things that are extraordinary become your day to day routine
- You're astounded how many French can fit into one vehicle
- Someone travelling with a washing machine makes you envious and little angry
- A microwave seems like a foreign object
- You start drooling over lamb grazing in a field

- Most of your arguments with your spouse are about how you're driving (& how lost you are)
- Waking up anywhere besides your tent, you're very disorientated
- One of your arms is tanned purple (Defender drivers)
- Your friends think you're permanently on holiday but you know they probably wouldn't last a week doing what you do
- You have "I Love" t-shirts from Mozambique, Peru and Mongolia
- You have left an array of expensive "great idea at the time" gadgets across continents
- In a year, you spend 11 months living outdoors
- Eating Western fast food is a grand, guilty treat
- You secretly consider yourself superior to backpackers and other "fly in" tourists
- Meeting other overlanders, driving the same vehicle, become instant family members
- You secretly worry that you might be developing a drinking problem
- You regularly make lifelong friends you will probably never see again
- Your children wash the dishes by hand and the laundry by foot
- You spend hours dreaming of ways to make money but hardly ever actually work
- When you do eventually work it is a 24 7, 365 marathon with the sole purpose of getting back on the road
- You get to know cities, bus routes, restaurants and the best supermarkets while looking for vehicle spare parts
- You won't know the date but you will know the countries exact exchange rate to the dollar
- You've eaten such strange food that your stomach is now lined by cast iron
- You realize coca-cola is available everywhere
- You lose huge amounts of weight eating the crappiest fatty food
- You have a strange relationship with your facial hair
- A box of chocolates seems like eating caviar
- You drink more beer than water
- Driving on tar you miss the dirt, when driving on dirt, you miss the tar
- When driving on a freeway makes you feel like you're driving in Formula One
- When the smell of a bushfire makes you hungry
- When fellow overlanders will hijack your Facebook post about visa requirements to discuss the condition of the road to Ulaanbataar
- When a conversation with a fellow overlander friend begins with "so, which country are you in these days"
- You have had so many late night chats sitting around the fire with incredibly wonderful and intelligent friends that you realise that the world is overflowing with good people, that governments, corporations and the media are the REAL problem and that the answer to most of the planets problems is a Scandinavian education. Knowledge is power!

about us

I am Graeme. I do the writing, driving, mechanical repairs and most of the cooking as well as helping out with the photographs and trying to build a social media following with our original content.

Luisa is the boss, she is always working and issuing instructions while coming up with new and excitingly tedious tasks for the family. Luisa is the principal photographer, organiser, navigator, penny counter and back seat driver.

Keelan is the first born. At age 18, he is 6 foot and a few hundred pounds, he should be back home playing rugby. Keelan is responsible for eating all the food, dinner dishes and doing all the heavy lifting, is a great assistant mechanic and spends his free time designing vehicles and structures.

Jessica is 13 apparently, I could swear she is 23. She takes care of her Dad and all the stray animals we meet, is in charge of breakfast and lunch dishes as well as helping out with the laundry. She is an aspiring Instagrammer. Both kids are homeschooled.

Luisa and I ran our own successful immigration firm in Cape Town, the most beautiful city in Africa. We were living the South African version of the American dream despite our terrible government and pathetic bureaucracy. We ate salmon and cream cheese, chilled in the pool, made a steak BBQ twice a week, had two PS3's, a Volvo station wagon and worked 14 hours a day. We had no head start in life and had to work persistently for every penny we earned.

**Our first book, We Will Be Free, well received and loved
available at www.a2aexpedition.com**

OVERLANDING THE AMERICAS

LA LUCHA

Graeme Bell

Our third book, Overlanding the Americas - La Lucha is the sequel to We Will Be Free available at www.a2aexpedition.com

Notes

Made in the USA
Columbia, SC
18 July 2018